CAREER IDEAS
for kids who like
MONEY

DIANE LINDSEY REEVES
WITH
GAYLE BRYAN

Illustrations by
NANCY BOND

Checkmark Books®
An imprint of Facts On File, Inc.

CAREER IDEAS FOR KIDS WHO LIKE MONEY

Checkmark Books
An imprint of Facts On File, Inc.
11 Penn Plaza
New York NY 10001

Library of Congress Cataloging-in-Publication Data

Reeves, Diane Lindsey, 1959–
    Career ideas for kids who like money / Diane Lindsey Reeves ;
with Gayle Bryan ; illustrations by Nancy Bond.
        p.   cm. — (Career ideas for kids)
    Includes bibliographical references and index.
    ISBN 0-8160-4319-1 (alk. paper) — ISBN 0-8160-4320-5 (pbk : alk. paper)
        1. Finance—Vocational guidance—Juvenile literature. 2. Financial
services industry—Vocational guidance—Juvenile literature. [1. Finance—
Vocational guidance. 2. Vocational guidance.] I. Bryan, Gayle. II. Bond,
Nancy, ill. III. Title.

HG173.8.R44 2001
332'.023'73—dc21   00-0059269

Text and cover design by Smart Graphics
Illustrations by Nancy Bond

This book is printed on acid-free paper.

Printed in the United States of America

MP FOF 10 9 8 7 6 5 4 3 2 1

(pbk)   10 9 8 7 6 5 4 3 2 1

To David,
Austin, and Abbie.

—GB

ACKNOWLEDGMENTS

A million thanks to the people who took the time to share
their career stories and provide photos for this book:

Cheryl Barnes
Charley Biggs
Bill Capodagli
Ronn Cordova
Bill Elsner
Donald Feinberg
Whit Friese
Joline Godfrey
Susan Gravely
Jennifer Hrometz
Nishat Karimi
Lynn Jackson
Joann Price
Leo Scrivner
Cynthia Tucker
Sylvia Varney

Also, special thanks to the design team of Smart Graphics,
Nancy Bond, and Cathy Rincon for bringing the
Career Ideas for Kids series to life with their creative talent.

Finally, much appreciation and admiration is due to
my editor, Nicole Bowen, whose vision and attention
to detail increased the quality of this project in
many wonderful ways.

CONTENTS

MAKE A CHOICE!

You're young. Most of your life is still ahead of you. How are you supposed to know what you want to be when you grow up?

You're right: 10, 11, 12, 13 is a bit young to know exactly what and where and how you're going to do whatever it is you're going to do as an adult. But, it's the perfect time to start making some important discoveries about who you are, what you like to do, and what you do best. It's the ideal time to start thinking about what you *want* to do.

Make a choice! If you get a head start now, you may avoid setbacks and mistakes later on.

When it comes to picking a career, you've basically got two choices.

CHOICE A

Wait until you're in college to start figuring out what you want to do. Even then you still may not decide what's up your alley, so you graduate and jump from job to job still searching for something you really like.

Hey, it could work. It might be fun. Lots of (probably most) people do it this way.

The problem is that if you pick Choice A, you may end up settling for second best. You may miss out on a meaningful education, satisfying work, and the rewards of a focused and well-planned career.

You have another choice to consider.

CHOICE B

Start now figuring out your options and thinking about the things that are most important in your life's work: Serving others? Staying true to your values? Making lots of money? Enjoying your work? Your young years are the perfect time to mess around with different career ideas without messing up your life.

Reading this book is a great idea for kids who choose B. It's a first step toward choosing a career that matches your skills, interests, and lifetime goals. It will help you make a plan for tailoring your junior and high school years to fit your career dreams. To borrow a jingle from the U.S. Army—using this book is a way to discover how to "be all that you can be."

Ready for the challenge of Choice B? If so, read the next section to find out how this book can help start you on your way.

HOW TO USE THIS BOOK

This isn't a book about interesting careers that other people have. It's a book about interesting careers that you can have.

Of course, it won't do you a bit of good to just read this book. To get the whole shebang, you're going to have to jump in with both feet, roll up your sleeves, put on your thinking cap—whatever it takes—to help you do these three things:

- 💡 **Discover** what you do best and enjoy the most. (This is the secret ingredient for finding work that's perfect for you.)

- 💡 **Explore** ways to match your interests and abilities with career ideas.
- 💡 **Experiment** with lots of different ideas until you find the ideal career. (It's like trying on all kinds of hats to see which ones fit!)

Use this book as a road map to some exciting career destinations. Here's what to expect in the chapters that follow.

GET IN GEAR!

First stop: self-discovery. These activities will help you uncover important clues about the special traits and abilities that make you *you*. When you are finished you will have developed a personal Skill Set that will help guide you to career ideas in the next chapter.

TAKE A TRIP!

Next stop: exploration. Cruise down the career idea highway and find out about a variety of career ideas that are especially appropriate for people who like math. Use the Skill Set chart at the beginning of each entry to match your own interests with those required for success on the job.

MAKE A DETOUR THAT COUNTS!

Here's your chance to explore up-and-coming opportunities in the business world, ways to be your own boss, and careers with higher than average earning potential.

Just when you thought you'd seen it all, here come dozens of moneymaking ideas to add to the career mix. Charge up your career search by learning all you can about some of these opportunities.

DON'T STOP NOW!

Third stop: experimentation. The library, the telephone, a computer, and a mentor—four keys to a successful career planning adventure. Use them well, and before long you'll be on the trail of some hot career ideas.

WHAT'S NEXT?

Make a plan! Chart your course (or at least the next stop) with these career planning road maps. Whether you're moving full steam ahead with a great idea or get slowed down at a yellow light of indecision, these road maps will keep you moving forward toward a great future.

Use a pencil—you're bound to make a detour or two along the way. But, hey, you've got to start somewhere.

HOORAY! YOU DID IT!

Some final rules of the road before sending you off to new adventures.

SOME FUTURE DESTINATIONS

This section lists a few career planning tools you'll want to know about.

You've got a lot of ground to cover in this phase of your career planning journey. Start your engines and get ready for an exciting adventure!

GET IN GEAR!

Career planning is a lifelong journey. There's usually more than one way to get where you're going, and there are often some interesting detours along the way. But, you have to start somewhere. So, rev up and find out all you can about you—one-of-a-kind, specially designed you. That's the first stop on what can be the most exciting trip of your life!

To get started, complete the two exercises described below.

WATCH FOR SIGNS ALONG THE WAY

Road signs help drivers figure out how to get where they want to go. They provide clues about direction, road conditions, and safety. Your career road signs will provide clues about who you are, what you like, and what you do best. These clues can help you decide where to look for the career ideas that are best for you.

Complete the following statements to make them true for you. There are no right or wrong answers. Jot down the response that describes you best. Your answers will provide important clues about career paths you should explore.

Please Note: If this book does not belong to you, write your responses on a separate sheet of paper.

On my last report card, I got the best grade in _____.

On my last report card, I got the worst grade in _____.

I am happiest when _____.

Something I can do for hours without getting bored is _____.

Something that bores me out of my mind is _____.

My favorite class is _____.

My least favorite class is _____.

The one thing I'd like to accomplish with my life is _____.

My favorite thing to do after school is __.

My least favorite thing to do after school is _____.

Something I'm really good at is _____.

Something that is really tough for me to do is _____.

My favorite adult person is _____ because _____.

When I grow up _____.

The kinds of books I like to read are about _____.

The kinds of videos I like to watch are about _____.

GET SOME DIRECTION

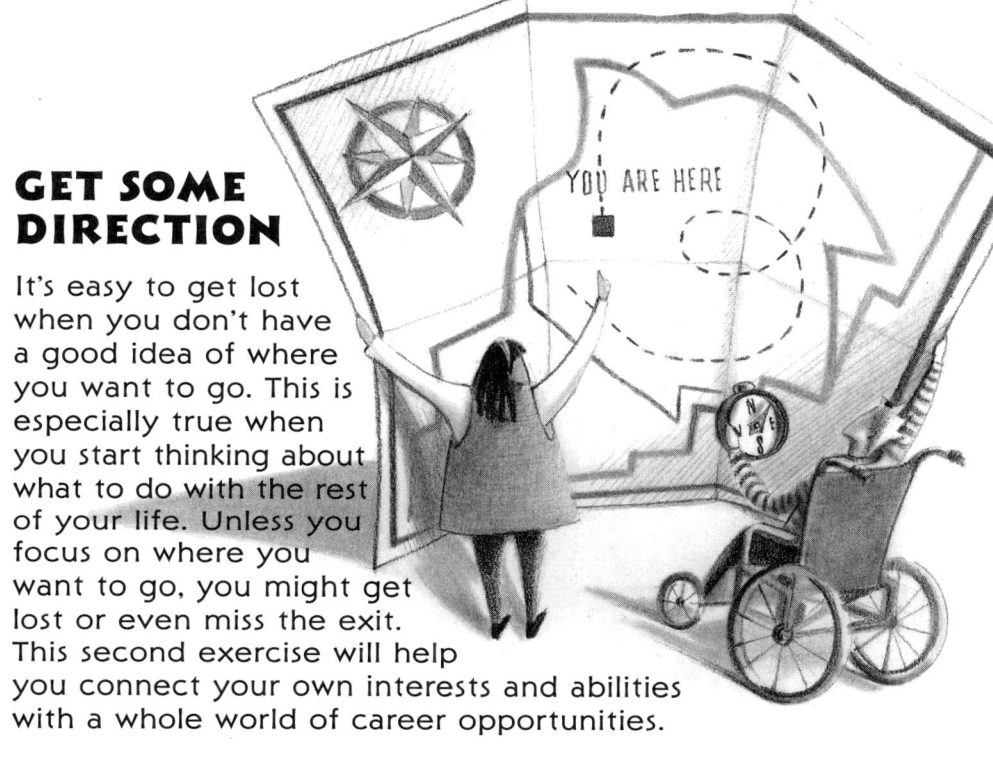

It's easy to get lost when you don't have a good idea of where you want to go. This is especially true when you start thinking about what to do with the rest of your life. Unless you focus on where you want to go, you might get lost or even miss the exit. This second exercise will help you connect your own interests and abilities with a whole world of career opportunities.

Mark the activities that you enjoy doing or would enjoy doing if you had the chance. Be picky. Don't mark ideas that you wish you would do, mark only those that you would really do. For instance, if the idea of skydiving sounds appealing, but you'd never do it because you are terrified of heights, don't mark it.

Please Note: If this book does not belong to you, write your responses on a separate sheet of paper.

❑ 1. Rescue a cat stuck in a tree
❑ 2. Visit the pet store every time you go to the mall
❑ 3. Paint a mural on the cafeteria wall
❑ 4. Send e-mail to a "pen pal" in another state
❑ 5. Survey your classmates to find out what they do after school
❑ 6. Run for student council
❑ 7. Try out for the school play
❑ 8. Dissect a frog and identify the different organs
❑ 9. Play baseball, soccer, football, or _____ (fill in your favorite sport)

❏ 10. Talk on the phone to just about anyone who will talk back

❏ 11. Try foods from all over the world—Thailand, Poland, Japan, etc.

❏ 12. Write poems about things that are happening in your life

❏ 13. Create a really scary haunted house to take your friends through on Halloween

❏ 14. Recycle all your family's trash

❏ 15. Bake a cake and decorate it for your best friend's birthday

❏ 16. Simulate an imaginary flight through space on your computer screen

❏ 17. Build model airplanes, boats, doll houses, or anything from kits

❏ 18. Sell enough advertisements for the school yearbook to win a trip to Walt Disney World

❏ 19. Teach your friends a new dance routine

❏ 20. Watch the stars come out at night and see how many constellations you can find

❏ 21. Watch baseball, soccer, football, or _____ (fill in your favorite sport) on TV

❏ 22. Give a speech in front of the entire school

❏ 23. Plan the class field trip to Washington, D.C.

❏ 24. Read everything in sight, including the back of the cereal box

❏ 25. Figure out "who dunnit" in a mystery story

❏ 26. Take in stray or hurt animals

❏ 27. Make a poster announcing the school football game

❏ 28. Put together a multimedia show for a school assembly using music and lots of pictures and graphics

❏ 29. Think up a new way to make the lunch line move faster and explain it to the cafeteria staff

❏ 30. Invest your allowance in the stock market and keep track of how it does

❏ 31. Go to the ballet or opera every time you get the chance

❏ 32. Do experiments with a chemistry set

❏ 33. Keep score at your sister's Little League game

- ❏ 34. Use lots of funny voices when reading stories to children
- ❏ 35. Ride on airplanes, trains, boats—anything that moves
- ❏ 36. Interview the new exchange student for an article in the school newspaper
- ❏ 37. Build your own treehouse
- ❏ 38. Help clean up a waste site in your neighborhood
- ❏ 39. Visit an art museum and pick out your favorite painting
- ❏ 40. Make a chart on the computer to show how much soda students buy from the school vending machines each week
- ❏ 41. Keep track of how much your team earns to buy new uniforms
- ❏ 42. Play Monopoly® in an all-night championship challenge
- ❏ 43. Play an instrument in the school band or orchestra
- ❏ 44. Put together a 1,000-piece puzzle
- ❏ 45. Write stories about sports for the school newspaper
- ❏ 46. Listen to other people talk about their problems
- ❏ 47. Imagine yourself in exotic places
- ❏ 48. Hang around bookstores and libraries
- ❏ 49. Play harmless practical jokes on April Fools' Day

❏ 50. Join the 4-H club at your school
❏ 51. Take photographs at the school talent show
❏ 52. Create an imaginary city using a computer
❏ 53. Do 3-D puzzles
❏ 54. Make money by setting up your own business—paper route, lemonade stand, etc.
❏ 55. Keep track of the top 10 songs of the week
❏ 56. Train your dog to do tricks
❏ 57. Make play-by-play announcements at the school football game
❏ 58. Answer the phones during a telethon to raise money for orphans
❏ 59. Be an exchange student in another country
❏ 60. Write down all your secret thoughts and favorite sayings in a journal
❏ 61. Jump out of an airplane (with a parachute, of course)
❏ 62. Plant and grow a garden in your backyard (or windowsill)
❏ 63. Use a video camera to make your own movies
❏ 64. Spend your summer at a computer camp learning lots of new computer programs
❏ 65. Build bridges, skyscrapers, and other structures out of LEGO®s

❏ 66. Get your friends together to help clean up your town after a hurricane

❏ 67. Plan a concert in the park for little kids

❏ 68. Collect different kinds of rocks

❏ 69. Help plan a sports tournament

❏ 70. Be DJ for the school dance

❏ 71. Learn how to fly a plane or sail a boat

❏ 72. Write funny captions for pictures in the school yearbook

❏ 73. Scuba dive to search for buried treasure

❏ 74. Recognize and name several different breeds of cats, dogs, and other animals

❏ 75. Sketch pictures of your friends

❏ 76. Answer your classmates' questions about how to use the computer

❏ 77. Draw a map showing how to get to your house from school

❏ 78. Pick out neat stuff to sell at the school store

❏ 79. Make up new words to your favorite songs

❏ 80. Take a hike and name the different kinds of trees, birds, or flowers

❏ 81. Referee intramural basketball games

❏ 82. Join the school debate team

❏ 83. Make a poster with postcards from all the places you went on your summer vacation

❏ 84. Write down stories that your grandparents tell you about when they were young

CALCULATE THE CLUES

Now is your chance to add it all up. Each of the 12 boxes on these pages contains an interest area that is common to both your world and the world of work. Follow these directions to discover your personal Skill Set:

1. Find all of the numbers that you checked on pages 9–13 in the boxes below and X them. Work your way all the way through number 84.
2. Go back and count the Xs marked for each interest area. Write that number in the space that says "total."
3. Find the interest area with the highest total and put a number one in the "Rank" blank of that box. Repeat this process for the next two highest scoring areas. Rank the second highest as number two and the third highest as number three.
4. If you have more than three strong areas, choose the three that are most important and interesting to you.

Remember: If this book does not belong to you, write your responses on a separate sheet of paper.

ADVENTURE
- ❏ 1
- ❏ 13
- ❏ 25
- ❏ 37
- ❏ 49
- ❏ 61
- ❏ 73
- Total: _____
- Rank: _____

ANIMALS & NATURE
- ❏ 2
- ❏ 14
- ❏ 26
- ❏ 38
- ❏ 50
- ❏ 62
- ❏ 74
- Total: _____
- Rank: _____

ART
- ❏ 3
- ❏ 15
- ❏ 27
- ❏ 39
- ❏ 51
- ❏ 63
- ❏ 75
- Total: _____
- Rank: _____

COMPUTERS

- ❑ 4
- ❑ 16
- ❑ 28
- ❑ 40
- ❑ 52
- ❑ 64
- ❑ 76

Total: _____
Rank: _____

MATH

- ❑ 5
- ❑ 17
- ❑ 29
- ❑ 41
- ❑ 53
- ❑ 65
- ❑ 77

Total: _____
Rank: _____

MONEY

- ❑ 6
- ❑ 18
- ❑ 30
- ❑ 42
- ❑ 54
- ❑ 66
- ❑ 78

Total: _____
Rank: _____

MUSIC/DANCE

- ❑ 7
- ❑ 19
- ❑ 31
- ❑ 43
- ❑ 55
- ❑ 67
- ❑ 79

Total: _____
Rank: _____

SCIENCE

- ❑ 8
- ❑ 20
- ❑ 32
- ❑ 44
- ❑ 56
- ❑ 68
- ❑ 80

Total: _____
Rank: _____

SPORTS

- ❑ 9
- ❑ 21
- ❑ 33
- ❑ 45
- ❑ 57
- ❑ 69
- ❑ 81

Total: _____
Rank: _____

TALKING

- ❑ 10
- ❑ 22
- ❑ 34
- ❑ 46
- ❑ 58
- ❑ 70
- ❑ 82

Total: _____
Rank: _____

TRAVEL

- ❑ 11
- ❑ 23
- ❑ 35
- ❑ 47
- ❑ 59
- ❑ 71
- ❑ 83

Total: _____
Rank: _____

WRITING

- ❑ 12
- ❑ 24
- ❑ 36
- ❑ 48
- ❑ 60
- ❑ 72
- ❑ 84

Total: _____
Rank: _____

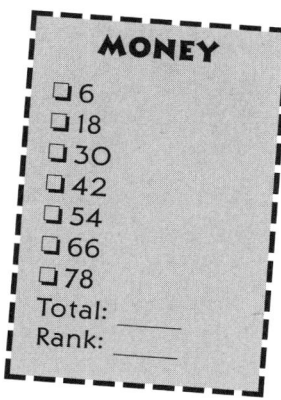
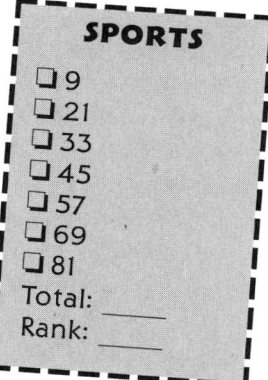

What are your top three interest areas? List them here (or on a separate piece of paper).

1. _____
2. _____
3. _____

WRITE YOUR RESPONSES ON A SEPARATE PIECE OF PAPER

This is your personal Skill Set and provides important clues about the kinds of work you're most likely to enjoy. Remember it and look for career ideas with a skill set that matches yours most closely.

TAKE A TRIP!

Cruise down the career idea highway and enjoy in-depth profiles of some of the interesting options in this field. Keep in mind all that you've discovered about yourself so far. Find the careers that match your own *Skill Set* first. After that, keep on trucking through the other ideas—exploration is the name of this game.

Let's get something straight first. Money isn't everything. It should never be the only reason to do something. You'll miss too much opportunity and are bound to wind up "poor" in other parts of your life if money is the only thing you're after. Got that?

OK. Then here's the thing: Money makes the world go 'round. Having some gives you more options to do what you want to do, live where you want to live, and do good things to help others.

If you can find a way to mix earning money with doing something that you really like to do, you'll have it made. When you look at people who have done this in a big way, you tend to see a couple of factors at play. Either they are doing something that involves lots of skill and expertise that other people will pay lots of money to get or they are doing something in an innovative way that creates new opportunity.

In the first category, you'll find people in more traditional types of big-bucks careers such as the law, medicine, banking, and the stock market. In the other category, you're more likely to find people with a bit of an entrepreneurial streak, people with good ideas and the guts to make them happen. Here you'll find innovative businesspeople, e-merchants, technology geeks, and the like.

Either way there are plenty of ways to make a good living financially while remaining true to yourself and all that you have to offer the world. Make sure you keep your priorities straight while you take a look at some of the following moneymaking career ideas.

Also, as you read about the following careers, imagine yourself doing each job and ask yourself the following questions:

- 💡 Would I like it?
- 💡 Would I be good at it?
- 💡 Is it the stuff my career dreams are made of?

If so, make a quick exit to explore what it involves, try it out, check it out, and get acquainted!

Buckle up and enjoy the trip!

A NOTE ON WEBSITES

Internet sites tend to move around the Web a bit. If you have trouble finding a particular site, use an Internet browser to find a specific website or type of information.

Advertising Executive

SKILL SET

✔ ART

✔ WRITING

✔ MONEY

WHAT IS AN ADVERTISING EXECUTIVE?

Just do it. Have it your way. When you care enough to send the very best. If you know that those slogans belong to Nike, Burger King, and Hallmark, it's because an advertising executive has done his or her job well. Companies like these spend more than $100 billion each year to get their names recognized and their products bought.

Advertising executives are the professionals they depend on to get the job done. Advertising executives generally possess a unique combination of artistic creativity and business savvy. They take the lead on advertising campaigns and projects. Sometimes ad execs may work primarily for one big client. Other times they work on a variety of smaller accounts. In either case the client is investing lots of money—sometimes millions of dollars—for advertising, and they expect a big return in increased name recognition and sales. Clients depend on advertising executives to deliver fresh, effective ideas in a professional, businesslike way.

Advertising executives spend their days schmoozing with clients, brainstorming ideas with other project team members, reviewing demographic research, and handling any of the zillions of details associated with an advertising campaign. The pace can be fast and intense.

New York and Chicago are considered two of the hot spots for advertising, and many of the major clients do business with big advertising firms with headquarters in these places. However, with increases in international advertising, you are just as likely to find branch offices in Bangkok, Thailand, as you are in Los Angeles, California. Along with the big firms, there are also growing numbers of smaller, and yes, entrepreneurial firms found just about anywhere. Although the common wisdom has these small firms handling more local accounts, they sometimes beat the big guys to the punch by presenting unique ideas and highly customized services to national clients.

Like any job, advertising has its pros and cons. On the plus side is the chance to let your creative juices flow. Advertising can be fun work, and seeing your work on TV, in magazines, and on billboards can be a real kick. There's lots of variety and plenty of challenge to keep things from getting boring too. On the downside is the continual need to please clients. Sometimes the client's idea of good advertising doesn't jibe with yours, but guess who wins? You got it. The client is always right and you better not forget it. There can also be a lot of stress associated with advertising because of tight deadlines. The hours can be long and the competition tough. But it can all be worth it when things come together and everybody starts noticing your work.

Other types of jobs found in the advertising agency include the following:

Account managers work as liaisons between the client and the advertising agency and make sure that everyone is working toward the same goals.

Copywriters, art directors, and creative directors are the people found in the creative departments of ad agencies—where ads are written and designed.

Production managers oversee the actual production of an advertising piece whether it is for radio, television, or some sort of print medium like a newspaper or magazine.

Media buyers are the people who find out how much various media costs and make the arrangements to buy advertising space. They are the ones who figure out the best mix of television, radio, newspaper, magazine, and other media for a specific advertising campaign. These decisions are far from guesswork. Instead they are based on lots of research.

While it almost always takes a degree in advertising, marketing, or some other business-related field to get your foot in the door at an advertising agency, there is only one thing that will keep you there: talent. An advertising executive is only as good as his or her last successful project. Creativity, fresh and innovative ideas, a way with words, and some artistic flair are what it takes to thrive in this exciting profession.

TRY IT OUT

GET YOUR BOOK TOGETHER

Something that all advertising professionals have in common is a portfolio, affectionately known as a "book." Depending on where they are in their careers, these books contain either storyboards from actual advertising campaigns they've worked on or, if they are new to the game, storyboards from advertising campaigns they wished they'd worked on. One of the best ways for you to find out if you'd like to make your career in advertising is to put your own book together.

All you need is a product, some great ideas, and a way to illustrate your ideas. First, pick a product that you really like—maybe a soft drink or a certain brand of sneakers. Next, think of the type of person most likely to buy that product and jot down ideas that might entice that audience to buy the product. Keep those ideas coming!

Finally, use markers, pictures cut from magazines, or computer graphics to put together your own ads. Try coming up with several different approaches for each product. Repeat this process several times and you'll have your first advertising "book" made up of fictitious campaigns for real products.

If you need some inspiration, try browsing through the following books:

Minsky, Lawrence, and Emily Thornton Calvo. *How to Succeed in Advertising When All You Have is Talent: Today's Top Creatives Show You How.* Lincolnwood, Ill.: NTC Publishing, 1996.

Paetro, Maxine, and Giff Crosby. *How to Put Your Book Together and Get a Job in Advertising.* Chicago: Copy Workshop, 1998.

Smith, Jeanette. *Breaking into Advertising. How to Market Yourself Like a Professional.* Princeton, N.J.: Peterson's Guides, 1998.

Sullivan, Luke. *Hey Whipple, Squeeze This: A Guide to Creating Great Ads.* New York: John Wiley, 1998.

THE WORD ON ADVERTISING

Speaking of books, here are some books that provide more information about careers in advertising.

Cotton, Stanley S. *Anybody Can Be in Advertising: It Beats Working for a Living.* Chicago: National Book Network, 1997.

Field, Shelly. *Career Opportunities in Advertising and Public Relations.* New York: Checkmark Books, 1997.

Ganim, Barbara A. *Approach an Advertising Agency and Walk Away with the Job You Want (Here's How).* Lincolnwood, Ill.: NTC Publishing Group, 1998.

Lederman, Eva. *Careers in Advertising.* New York: Princeton Review, 1999.

HOT OFF THE PRESS

For the absolutely latest news in advertising visit Adweek Online at http://www.adweek.com. It's the place ad execs go to find out who's who and what's what in advertising. Be sure to look at the Best Spots pages. That's where the professionals spotlight the best new ads.

ADVERTISING FOR WORK

If you really want to know what kinds of opportunities are out there, fast forward your life about 10 years or so and pretend that you are a recent college graduate looking for a lucky break in advertising. You won a college advertising competition and worked as an intern for an ad agency for two summers. With that scenario in mind, see what kinds of jobs you'd qualify for at websites such as:

http://www.ad-pros.com
http://www.AdAge.com
http://www.CareerMart.com
http://www.jwtworld.com

ADVERTISING 101

Want a quick lesson in how the advertising game is played? Look at the websites of some of America's top advertising agencies and see how they advertise themselves. First, make a list of the following companies and rate their performance. Make sure to jot down a few notes about why you do (or don't) like their approach. Here are websites for the some of the biggest and best ad firms:

BBDO Worldwide   http://www.bbdo.com
D'Arcy Masius   http://www.dmbb.com
DDB Needham   http://www.ddbn.com
Foote Cone & Belding   http://www.fcb.com
J. Walter Thompson   http://www.jwt.com
Leo Burnett   http://www.leoburnett.com
Ogilvy & Mather   http://www.ogilvy.com
Saatchi & Saatchi   http://www.saatchi-saatchi.com
Young & Rubicam   http://www.youngandrubicam.com

AND THE WINNER IS . . .

Movies have the Oscars, music has the Grammys, and advertising has the Clio Awards. It's a BIG deal to win a Clio. Take a look at the latest winners and see what you think of them. Are they really the cream of the crop or just overdone flops? Catch all the excitement at http://www.clioawards.com.

CYBER FIELD TRIP

Here's one museum you can tour from the comfort of your computer chair. Find it at http://www.prmuseum.com and see if you agree that it is "the place to go to learn about how ideas are developed for industry, education, and government, and how they have been applied to successful public relations programs since the PR industry was born."

CHECK IT OUT

The Ad Council
261 Madison Avenue
New York, New York 10016-2302
http://www.adcouncil.com

American Advertising Federation
1101 Vermont Avenue NW, Suite 500
Washington, D.C. 20005
http://www.aaf.org

American Association of Advertising Agencies
405 Lexington Avenue, 18th Floor
New York, New York 10174
http://www.aaaa.org

American Marketing Association
311 S. Wacker Drive, Suite 5800
Chicago, Illinois 60606
http://www.ama.org

Association of National Advertisers
155 East 44th Street
New York, New York 10017
http://www.ana.net

International Advertising Association
521 Fifth Avenue, Suite 1807
New York, New York 10175
http://www.iaaglobal.org

Public Relations Society of America
33 Irving Place
New York, New York 10003-2376
http://www.prsa.org

GET ACQUAINTED

Whit Friese,
Advertising Executive

CAREER PATH

CHILDHOOD ASPIRATION: To be a professional football player.

FIRST JOB: Working at a miniature golf course.

CURRENT JOB: Creative director and vice president at Leo Burnett.

FATHER KNOWS BEST

Like a lot of young boys, Whit Friese wanted to play professional football when he grew up. The problem was that he didn't grow up quite big enough to make it as a pro. As a six-foot-tall and 165-pound high school junior, he started looking into other options. His dad happened to notice that Friese had a doodling habit—he drew goofy little drawings on everything he could get his hands on. Friese's dad must have thought the doodles were pretty good because one day he brought home for his son a book about careers in advertising. The book got Friese interested enough to pursue a degree in advertising at Pennsylvania State University.

While in college, Friese took a lot of art classes that allowed him to cultivate his creative design skills. By the time he graduated from college, he was sure that he wanted to work on the creative side of advertising. He put his book together so he could show prospective employers what he could do with different kinds of products, headed back home to Chicago, and started hunting for a job.

A LUCKY BREAK . . . EVENTUALLY

Friese was a little disappointed that the advertising world didn't immediately welcome him with open arms. He took his book around to several big firms, but all had the same basic response: "Thanks, but no thanks." So Friese sold ads for a newspaper for about eight months until his job prospects took a definite turn for the better.

It wasn't just luck that turned things around. It was a winning combination of hard work and pure talent. Add just a dash of courage and you have the recipe for Friese's big splash into the advertising world. Instead of sitting around waiting for ad agencies to call, he looked for a way to get their attention. He entered an ad he designed in a national contest—and won. Several newspapers carried the story, and the story was seen by the powers that be at Leo Burnett, one of the biggest ad firms around. Someone realized they had Friese's book on file and gave him a call. As a result, he landed a plum position as an art director for the prestigious firm.

IT'S THE REAL THING

Now several years and many successful ad campaigns later, Friese is creative director for the world's largest soft drink company. It's an account that takes him all over the world to places such as South Africa, India, Japan, and Europe to develop campaigns that fit with these various cultures.

Friese is in charge of a team of six people who work exclusively on this account at Leo Burnett. Together the team is constantly brainstorming, looking for the next big thing. They keep an eye on fashion, art, magazines, and music to keep up with the latest trends and fads. They also do some hard-core research into the product, the target market, and each city and country that they work in. All this work plays a part in pitching their client's product in an entertaining and memorable way.

A CONFESSION AND SOME ADVICE

Friese is the first to admit that he loves his job. He loves it so much, in fact, that it is not unusual for him to spend several hours at the office on Sunday just because he wants to be there.

He says that some of the best advice he's gotten came from his parents. They told him that if he really wanted to get into advertising, he could do it. They said that even if he had to take a few lumps along the way, it would be worth it. So far, they've been right.

Business Manager

SKILL SET

✔ MONEY
✔ COMPUTERS
✔ TALKING

WHAT IS A BUSINESS MANAGER?

Business managers come in all shapes and sizes. They are just as likely to work for a huge corporation as they are for a small company. They work for many types of businesses including accounting, banking, insurance, real estate, marketing, retail, public relations, manufacturing, and entertainment companies. They may be responsible for managing a few or a few thousand employees.

Managers are best known as the "boss" of a given company, division, or project. To put it simply, a manager's job is to decide what needs to be done and to make sure that it gets done right. This responsibility almost always means that a big part of a manager's job is getting other people to do their jobs.

The people part of the job is a big one. Managers are often responsible for hiring and firing, motivating their workers to be productive and efficient, making sure everyone has the skills and resources they need to do their jobs, and keeping peace among the ranks. To get a basic idea of what this can involve, multiply the number of people in your family by 10

28

and think about what it would be like to manage all of their schedules and handle all of their problems.

In addition to managing people, a business manager often is responsible for managing the finances of his or her department, division, or project. This can involve setting budgets and monitoring the resources of the group.

Managers also often find themselves in the middle: they have bosses above them whom they must please and they have workers below them whom they have to keep happy. It's like playing monkey in the middle. Balancing the two is best done by providing good information both up and down the company ladder. Good communication skills are a must for any kind of business manager.

All these aspects—the people, the finances, and the information—come together to achieve a certain goal. Manufacturing a product or providing a service is what a business manager is ultimately responsible to do.

Education and experience are two ways to prepare to become a business manager. Many business managers have college degrees in business administration, accounting, finance, or some other business-related subject. A master's degree in business administration, known as an MBA, is often seen as crucial to moving ahead in business. However, college is generally only the beginning of the educational

process. On-the-job training and ongoing specialized training are both necessary for most business managers.

Companies looking for newly graduated, inexperienced managers are few and far between. Instead, would-be managers may be given responsibility as supervisors, managers in training, or other types of "just getting started" positions. To become a business manager, be ready to start at the bottom of the business ladder, pay your dues, and work your way up through the ranks.

Strong leadership and an ability to make things happen are desirable skills in all types of industries. And since the world is turning toward a global economy, any international experience you gain can only help your chances for advancement.

Make sure that you set aside any preconceived notions of stepping on other people on the way to success. While a certain amount of competitiveness is a part of the business world, cutthroat tactics are more likely to be part of a television movie than they are a business you'd want to work for. People who genuinely like people, who can clearly communicate good ideas, who build supportive networks of mutually beneficial relationships, and who really like their work are the most likely to succeed in management.

Once you reach the level of general manager or top executive—with titles such as chief executive officer, executive vice president, owner, partner, or chief—you'll be working among the highest paid workers in the country. Six-figure salaries plus stock options, dividends, bonuses, and other perks are not unusual for experienced business managers. How does that sound as an investment in your future?

TRY IT OUT

JOIN THE BEST OF THE BEST

Every year, *Fortune* magazine lists the top 500 money-making businesses in America. You can find links to these corporate hotshots at http://www.pathfinder.com/fortune/

fortune500. Take a look at the list and see how many companies you recognize.

Make your own list of the top companies you do business with. Your list might include a fast-food chain or two, your favorite clothes companies, sports equipment manufacturers, and the like.

BUSINESS BASICS

Following are some books on business that will give you an idea of some of the opportunities that may await you.

Beatty, Richard H., and Nicholas C. Burholder. *The Executive Career Guide for MBAs: Inside Advice for Getting to the Top from Today's Business Leaders.* New York: John Wiley, 1995.

Butler, Timothy, and James Waldroop. *Discovering Your Career In Business.* New York: Perseus Press, 1997.

Hamadeh, H. S., and Andy Richard. *Business School Companion: The Ultimate Guide to Excelling in Business School and Launching Your Career.* New York: Princeton Review, 1995.

Peterson's Job Opportunities for Business Majors. Princeton, N.J.: Peterson's, 1999.

MANAGEMENT 101

If you decide to pursue a career in management, don't overlook this simple fact: the most important person you must learn to manage is you. Start your management training with the following book and companion journal. This is one "homework" assignment you'll be glad you did.

Covey, Sean. *The 7 Habits of Highly Effective Teens: The Ultimate Teenage Success Guide.* New York: Simon and Schuster, 1998.

Covey, Sean, and Debra Harris. *The 7 Habits of Highly Effective Teens Journal.* Salt Lake City, Utah: Franklin Covey, 1999.

BUSINESS PLAYGROUND

If you've got a pair of dice, a deck of cards, paper, a pencil, and a couple of friends, you've got all you need to have some fun learning about business. Go to the Business Games website at http://www.icon.co.za/~zapr to find instructions for:

- ☼ Middleman, a game of supply and demand.
- ☼ Card Stock Market, a game dealing with share investment and price manipulation.
- ☼ Showbiz, a game simulating shifting public taste.

EXPERIENCE ALWAYS HELPS

It's not necessary to wait until you are an adult to get some experience in business. Start now by getting a paper route, managing a sports team at school, or getting involved in student government. You'll learn lots about leadership and what it takes to keep an organization running smoothly.

You may even find a way to make a few bucks in the process. How about setting up a refreshment stand at the local soccer or baseball field? Anywhere there are hungry or thirsty people will do. Serve lemonade, soft drinks, snacks, or whatever. Just make sure that you get permission first.

DRESS FOR SUCCESS

Find out all you need to know about looking like a successful businessperson with an on-line magazine called MBA Style. Here you'll find fashion and interview tips and links to many other sites of interest to up-and-coming business managers. It's a fun site you'll want to see. Find it at http://www.mbastyle.com.

CHECK IT OUT

American Management Association
1601 Broadway
New York, New York 10019
http://www.amanet.org

Institute of Management and Administration
29 West 35th Street
New York, New York 10001-2299
http://www.ioma.com

National Management Association
2210 Arbor Boulevard
Dayton, Ohio 45439-1580
http://nam1.org

U.S. Chamber of Commerce
1615 H Street NW
Washington, D.C. 20062
http://www.uschamber.com

GET ACQUAINTED

Leo Scrivner,
Business Manager

CAREER PATH

CHILDHOOD ASPIRATION: To be a cowboy.

FIRST JOB: Selling Popsicles to workers on his family's ranch.

CURRENT JOB: Director of human resources for Motorola's Worldwide Supply Chain Operation and Employee Relations

HOME ON THE RANGE

Leo Scrivner was born and raised on a ranch in northern Mexico, so it was only natural that his boyhood dream was to be a cowboy. Just give him a horse, some rope, and a herd of cows, and he'd be happy. This dream held until he got old enough to drive and he traded horses for wheels. Then he started toying with the idea of taking to the road in one of those big 18-wheel trucks.

Neither of these ideas thrilled his parents. They wanted Scrivner to go to law school. But Scrivner wasn't even remotely interested in becoming a lawyer. So he found a way to go to college without having to depend on his parents or anyone else for help. He was accepted at the United States Military Academy (USMA) in West Point, New York. Instead of paying to attend college at West Point, the government pays the tuition and graduates owe Uncle Sam at least four years of military service instead.

YOU'RE IN THE ARMY NOW

Once settled in at West Point, Scrivner found he liked playing "soldier." After four years of hard work and challenging training, it was "duty, honor, country" all the way for Scrivner.

After graduating, the newly commissioned Lieutenant Scrivner was assigned to an army post in Germany. He knew he was in the real army as soon as he got off the airplane: he was given a flak jacket and a loaded .45, and put on a high-level alert for counterterrorist activity.

As if that wasn't enough, about a month later he received an early morning phone call that put all his military training to the test. It seems that during the night someone had lowered a five-gallon load of explosives through a hole in the roof of Scrivner's barracks. Luckily someone discovered the bomb before it was set to go off. Good thing Scrivner had paid attention in class! All the stuff he'd learned from books came together to help defuse the crisis that day.

HELLO, CIVILIAN WORLD

Eight years of working for Uncle Sam proved enough for Scrivner. After successfully serving as company commander for a mechanized infantry unit, he was ready to try something new. So he traded in his camouflage uniform for a suit and tie and went to work for a major Fortune 500 company.

Scrivner was pleasantly surprised to discover how well his military experience translated into the corporate world. The army had taught him to look at tough situations and figure out the best ways to deal with them. It taught him how to work with all kinds of people. And it taught him to look beyond the obvious and be prepared for all the "what ifs" that seem to have a way of popping up when you least expect them. With these skills under his belt, Scrivner was ready to go to work as a business manager specializing in training and human resources.

A WORLD OF OPPORTUNITY

Even Scrivner's boyhood days on the ranch in Mexico came in handy. The company he worked for needed a Spanish-speaking manager to open a new factory in Mexico and head up the Latin American operations.

Now Scrivner's work takes him all over the world to places such as Singapore, China, Korea, Brazil, Mexico, Ireland, Scotland, and Germany. Scrivner calls this part of his job "space shuttle diplomacy," and it's not unusual for him to go all around the globe in just 10 days—often spending as many nights sleeping on an airplane as he does in a hotel.

A WORD TO THE WISE

So what does Scrivner have to say to kids like you who hope to someday succeed in business? In a word: education. Get some. Take the hard courses and challenge yourself. He says the more education you get now, the more choices you'll have later. More choices means more fun on the job. That's because you won't get stuck doing something you don't like because you can't do anything else.

Chief Technology Officer

WHAT IS A CHIEF TECHNOLOGY OFFICER?

Chief technology officers are in charge of the information and technology aspects of a company. Sounds simple enough until you start describing what an information system involves. A computer information system includes the analysis, design, development, and implementation of systems that record, transmit, store, and process information. It includes business, scientific, mathematical, and industrial control systems, and it emphasizes software applications. If being a chief technology officer sounds like a complicated job, that's because it is. It's complicated and challenging and always on the cutting edge.

Companies of all shapes and sizes depend on their chief technology officers (sometimes called chief information officers or CIOs) to know how to use technology and information systems to make their businesses more efficient, productive, and profitable. Companies rely on their CTOs to provide the high-tech expertise they need to stay competitive in the business world. CTOs can be responsible for thousands, even millions, of dollars worth of equipment. In a day and age where the efficient use of technology can literally make or break a business, the company has a lot riding on the CTO's success.

It's highly unlikely that you'll begin your career as a chief technology officer. There are lessons to be learned and dues to be paid. Typical career paths include computer programmers who work their way up to the position of CTO or business managers who make the switch to technology. Either way, it's important to understand technology and business in order to handle the dual responsibilities of this type of senior level executive position.

Business schools around the country have responded to growing needs for well-trained CTOs by offering business degrees with an emphasis in information systems as well as degrees in information systems with an emphasis in business. This is a trend that is expected to continue as colleges and universities try to keep pace with technological advances.

The Internet offers another way to combine business and technology on your way up to the top job. Opportunities for managers of Internet and Intranet technologies are booming. Quite often, these types of positions are filled by younger, technically savvy computer types.

Though the levels of responsibility may vary quite a bit among the top positions and these types of managerial slots, there are some similarities in types of skills used to do the job. All the tasks generally associated with management—attending

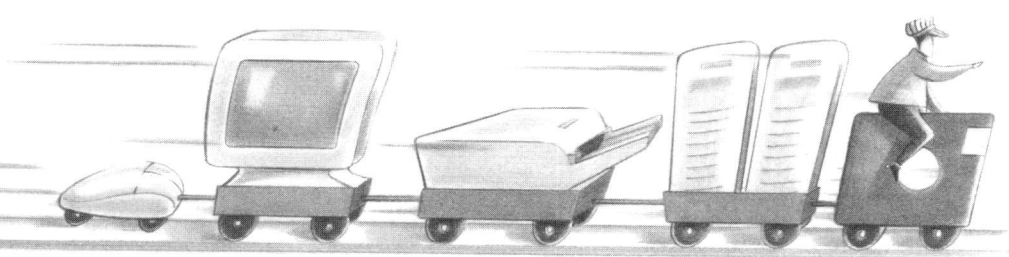

meetings, writing reports, working with budgets, supervising other people—are coupled with applying technology to meet a company's goals and priorities.

Right now the information technology market is hot. To succeed, you'll need to be well-rounded. It's one thing to be a computer geek and another thing to be a computer geek with an edge. Learning how to think, how to analyze situations, how to communicate clearly, how to work in a team—these are the types of skills that will work for you no matter what programming language you're "speaking" or what new-fangled technology you use.

TRY IT OUT

COMPUTER WHIZ KID

If you see computers in your future, you'd better make sure they are a big part of your present. Take advantage of every opportunity you get to learn your way around computers. Play computer games, and even learn to create your own computer games. Three good places to start are:

- Kidscom website at http://www.kidscom.com
- Knowledge Adventure website at http://www.adventure.com/kids/games
- Game Writers Page at http://game.ncl.ac.uk (this is the real stuff)

Learn the lingo of programming. Better yet, learn to program. Two good places to start are:

- The Kids and Computers website at http://www.magma.ca/~dsleeth
- The Great Logo Adventure website at http://members.home.net/tgla

Take computer classes at school. In addition, take advantage of some of the resources on the Internet to learn about things you really want to know about. Two good places to start are:

- ☼ Rules of the Road website at http://www.usdoj.gov/kidspage/dodont/kidinternet.htm
- ☼ Computer Lessons for Kids and Small Adults website at http://www2.magmacom.com/~dsleeth/kids/lessons/starter.htm

HOMEMADE HARDWARE

There is no better way to get acquainted with a computer than to build your own PC. Go ahead and give it a try. Step-by-step instructions can be found at http://www.verinet.com/pc.

CAREERS THAT COMPUTE

There are lots of ways to center your career on computers and technology. Take a look at some of these books for more ideas.

Burns, J. K. *Opportunities in Computer Systems Careers.* Lincolnwood, Ill.: VGM Career Horizons, 1996.

Eberts, Marjorie, and M. Gisler. *Careers for Computer Buffs and Other Technological Types.* Lincolnwood, Ill.: VGM Career Horizons, 1994.

Henderson, Harry. *Career Opportunities in Computers and Cyberspace.* New York: Checkmark Books, 1999.

Morgan, B. J., and J. M. Palmisano. *Computing and Software Design Career Directory.* Detroit: Visible Ink Press, 1993.

Morris, Mary, and Paul Maissie. *Cybercareers.* Mountain Valley, Calif.: Sun Microsystems, 1998.

CHECK IT OUT

Association of Information Technology Professionals
315 South Northwest Highway, Suite 200
Park Ridge, Illinois 60068
http://www.aitp.org

Association of Women in Computing
41 Sutter Street, Suite 1006
San Francisco, California 94104
http://www.awc-hq.org

IEEE Computer Society
1730 Massachusetts Avenue NW
Washington, D.C. 20036-1992
http://www.ieee.com

Information and Technology Association of America
1616 North Fort Meyer Drive, Suite 1300
Arlington, Virginia 22209
http://www.itaa.org

Institute for Operations Research and Management Sciences
901 Elridge Landing Road, Suite 400
Linthicom, Maryland 21090-2909
http://www.informs.org

GET ACQUAINTED

Donald Feinberg,
Chief Technology Officer

CAREER PATH

CHILDHOOD ASPIRATION: To be a physicist because his father wanted him to be a "real" scientist.

FIRST JOB: Programmer for Wang Laboratories.

CURRENT JOB: Chief technology officer for Student Online, a higher education Intranet portal company.

CURIOSITY AND THE KID

Things were different when Donald Feinberg was a boy. His family didn't have a lot of money, and back then there weren't software games and computers to spend it on anyway. So, Feinberg entertained himself by building his own radio equipment. He rode around town on his bike looking for castaway television parts. Feinberg credits this experience in "learning how to learn" as the best preparation he got for his career in technology.

Feinberg uses the following example to describe the kind of kid he was. He says his family lived near Coney Island, a famous amusement park in New York, and his parents often took him there to enjoy the rides. However, he remembers that from as early as four or five years old, he never rode the carousel horse sitting up like the other kids. Instead, he was always bent over looking at all the pulleys and gears trying to figure out how the ride worked.

Now Feinberg realizes that this insatiable curiosity and penchant for making things meant he was a "real engineer." These interests helped shape his intellect and how he looks at problems in ways he could never have learned in an engineering class.

Feinberg admits that he's afraid this intellectual building process gets lost today, now that kids have access to all kinds of flashy computer equipment and high-tech entertainment activities. He worries that they don't learn how to think for themselves and that the creative genius that has made this country great may vanish.

ON THE CUTTING EDGE

Feinberg started working with computers sort of by accident. On the advice of his father, who believed that studying the hard sciences was better than engineering, Feinberg went to college to become a physicist. He completed a bachelor's degree, a master's degree, and was halfway through a doctorate program when he realized that he hated every minute of it. What he really liked was his job as a graduate assistant, which involved programming computers for some of his professors. He never took a computer science course but was just naturally good at figuring out how to make them work. Working with computers, not physics, is how he has made his living ever since.

And it's a good thing for all of us that he made the switch because Feinberg is credited with inventing the CD-ROM. This exciting development came about as a way to solve a problem for his employer, a software manufacturing company called Digital. The company was enjoying great success in developing software that was in big demand. In fact, the demand for these products was so great that the company couldn't keep up with it. That's because they had to use a computer to replicate each program one by one. It took a lot of time and a lot of computer equipment to produce software kits this way.

Feinberg knew that the music industry had started recording music on compact disks. He knew there had to be a way to use a similar process to "record" computer programming on them as well. At first, he was about the only one who thought it was possible—everyone else said it couldn't be done. It took about two and a half years and lots of trial and error to prove them wrong. The process was so complicated that his team of engineers even had to develop new equipment to make it work.

Eventually the hard work paid off and Feinberg was a hero, even though he didn't realize it at the time. Feinberg says that he had no idea how this discovery would revolutionize technology and have a great impact on the world.

MAKING WAVES

Through the years, Feinberg has worked on projects all over the world. He's worked in the space industry and has the opportunity to work on an amazing variety of projects. He is especially proud to have been a part of the political transition in Poland in the early 1990s. He made approximately 200 trips to the country within four years, and he was able to influence many major projects and clients in the use of technology in that emerging democracy.

Feinberg is the first to admit that his unorthodox approach to solving problems is not always welcome. He says that some people refuse to hire him because he's always trying to change things. Feinberg's response? "You can't make an omelette without breaking some eggs!"

In his present position as CTO, he leads a team of computer engineers to develop products and services for use in colleges and universities. He says it is a challenge to stay a step ahead of his people, but he usually manages by doing a lot of planning and reading and always looking for a better way to do something.

YOU HEARD IT HERE FIRST

Feinberg says the best thing a future chief technology officer can do to prepare for the job is to learn how to think! He believes that there is no substitute for just doing things. Forget the fancy computer gadgets that come straight from the store. See what you can make with a tin can and a little ingenuity.

E-Merchant

WHAT IS AN E-MERCHANT?

E-merchants sell products over the Internet. Such businesses allow customers to shop from their own homes at any time of day or night and have their purchases delivered to their doorstep.

E-commerce is a new way of doing business that didn't even exist just a few years ago. But it's a concept that's taken off. Super e-merchants (also known as e-tailers) like Amazon.com and eToys.com have taken the retail business by storm. Consumers spent $2.8 billion dollars over the Internet in the month of January 2000 alone. That's a lot of cash! This has made the retail industry sit up and take notice. Even favorite retailers you find in "real" malls are starting to set up shop on the web. Toys"R"Us, Barnes and Noble, and the Gap are just a few of the traditional retailers jumping on the Internet bandwagon. Then again, so are thousands of entrepreneurial types who see an opportunity in the making and are joining in on the fun.

What does it take to be an e-merchant? First, you have to have something to sell. It could be books, toys, clothes, computer software, airline tickets, music, or anything else you can think of. Next, you have to open a cyberstore. Not like the ones you find at the mall, but one that exists only on-line (and in your basement or wherever you keep your products).

The big challenge is in finding customers. To do this, you have to advertise and make your presence on the Internet known.

One of the first techniques successful e-merchants use to attract business is to make it easy for customers to buy their goods. You have to be able to accept payments on-line, which means credit cards. You have to provide your customers with a secure way to send you their credit card information on-line. When you get orders, you have to fill them and ship them out. And, finally, you have to offer customer service in case things don't go exactly right.

As you can imagine, there are many different career opportunities available in e-commerce. Some entrepreneurs might take on the whole project. They might have a product or products they wish to sell, set up their own website, and go for it. But the chances are remote that any one person has all the skills and time necessary to run an on-line store alone. So a successful business might require partners or hiring others with complimentary skill sets. For example,

you might be a computer whiz who can design an incredible on-line store, process payments, and make sure credit card transactions are secure. Then you might enlist help from someone with some retail or customer service expertise.

No matter what, make sure you choose a product that people will want to buy. Some e-merchants have gotten so excited about the technology and the possibilities of selling over the Internet that they have paid little attention to what they are selling. You can have the world's greatest website and get 50,000 hits a day, but if you don't have a product worth buying, you won't be in business for long.

If going it alone is not for you, there are many different job opportunities in this growing field. If you scanned employment ads in e-commerce publications, you would find technical job listings such as Internet product development and technology analyst, e-commerce technology architecture manager, e-commerce applications developers, or e-commerce infrastructure managers. These are all technical jobs that require heavy computer experience in web development and maintenance. Some jobs may require a B.S. degree and some may require lots of experience with computer languages such as HTML, JavaScript, PDF, and Visual Basic, among others. Some might require both.

A position like that of Internet business development manager might require a marketing or business degree and would involve research and development of sales and marketing strategies for a large e-commerce company. A director of e-commerce would probably need computer and business experience as well as an advanced degree such as an MBA.

Because e-commerce is such a new and evolving field, there is not one obvious choice for an education. Colleges and universities themselves are debating how to best educate their students for careers in e-commerce. Some universities offer e-commerce programs through their computer science and information science divisions. Degree programs, both undergraduate and graduate, are starting to crop up at business schools around the country such as the University of Texas, Duke, and Harvard. They are starting to realize that

their students need to have diverse backgrounds in computers and business to succeed in e-commerce. With that said, a college degree is not necessarily a requirement for an e-commerce career, especially if you are great with computers.

Keep your eye on e-commerce. It is so new and is changing so quickly that you never know what exciting careers may yet develop.

TRY IT OUT

SURF WITH THE PROS

Check out the websites of three major e-tailers on-line: Amazon.com (http://www.amazon.com), eToys (http://www.etoys.com), and Lands' End (http://www.landsend.com).

Surf with a purpose. Make notes about how these sites are organized. What do they have in common? What makes them stand out? What is it about their look that is special? Are they easy to navigate? Fill your virtual shopping cart and go through the process of placing an order. Was it easy to understand? Did it take too long? Would you feel safe sending them your credit card information on-line?

GOING, GOING, GONE!

One way to get your feet wet in e-commerce without investing a lot of time or money is through an auction site like e-Bay. People buy and sell thousands of products a day on e-Bay, ranging from computers to vintage Barbie dolls. Visit the site at http://www.ebay.com and read all the information about selling and bidding on auction items.

Maybe you collect baseball cards or have a piece of sports equipment that you don't use and would be interested in putting up for auction. Do this only with your parents' permission and help. You will be responsible for collecting the money from your buyer and shipping the buyer your product. This could be a valuable lesson in e-commerce and you may make a little money to boot.

SPIN A WEB

Test your computer savvy by taking an on-line tutorial on web design at http://hotwired.lycos.com/webmonkey/index. html. Then visit http://angelfire.com for more information about building and posting it for free.

SEE THE SITES

You guessed it—the best place to get more information about e-commerce is on the Web. Here are some sites worth visiting:

E-Commerce Times at http://www.E-Commercetimes.com has up-to-date e-commerce news from around the world.

Find out how to build a successful on-line business at the E-Commerce Advisor's site at http://www.sotkin.com.

e-Commerce @lert at http://www.zdjournals.com says they are your complete source for electronic commerce analysis strategy, and interaction. They have lots of information worth checking out.

To search for an e-commerce business course, visit http://E-Commerce.miningco.com/smallbusiness/ E-Commerce/msub31.htm.

If you would like to browse through e-commerce job listings, visit http://E-Commerce.miningco.com/smallbusiness/E-Commerce/msub4.htm.

Sell It on the Web at http://www.sellitontheweb.com has an E-Commerce 101 (that means the basics) section as well as new technology and Web store reviews.

The E-Commerce Info Center at http://ecominfocenter. com is another comprehensive site that has lots of links to all sorts of e-commerce sites.

The E-Commerce Guidebook at http://www.online-commerce.com is an on-line guide for learning the e-commerce business.

The Center for Web Understanding at http://www. webcen.com has compiled Web information and resources to help you understand and use the Web effectively.

HIT THE BOOKS
Check out some of these e-commerce books to get more information about this new and exciting field.

Birch, Alex, Dirk Schneider, and Philip Gerbert. *The Age of E-Tail: Conquering the New World of Electronic Shopping.* Minneapolis: Capstone Book Press, 2000.

Cunningham, Mike. *Smart Things to Know About E-Commerce.* Minneapolis: Capstone Publishing, 1999.

Kalakota, Ravi, Don Tapscott, and Marcia Robinson. *E-Business: Roadmap for Success.* Reading, Mass.: Addison Wesley Longman, 1999.

Korper, Steffano, and Juanita Ellis. *The E-Commerce Book: Building the E-Empire.* San Diego: Academic Press, 1999.

McLaren, Bruce J., and Constance H. McLaren. *E-Commerce: Business on the Internet.* New York: Intrepid Traveller Publications, 1999.

Siebel, Thomas M., and Pat House. *Cyber Rules: Strategies for Excelling at E-Business.* New York: Doubleday, 1999.

Smith, Rob S., Mark Thompson, and Mark Speaker. *The Complete Idiot's Guide to e-Commerce.* Minneapolis: Que, 2000.

Tiernan, Bernadette. *E-tailing.* Chicago: Dearborn Financial Publishing, 1999.

CHECK IT OUT

CommerceNet
10050 North Wolfe Road,
    Suite SW2-2255
Cupertino, California 95014
http://www.commerce.net.com

National Retail Federation
E-Commerce Division
325 7th Street NW, Suite 1100
Washington, D.C. 20004
http://www.nrf.com

GET ACQUAINTED

Charley Biggs, E-Merchant

CAREER PATH

CHILDHOOD ASPIRATION: To be either a professional tennis player or Superman.

FIRST JOB: Cutting lawns and giving tennis lessons.

CURRENT JOB: Chief Operating Officer, Ecamps.com.

SPORTS WITH A TWIST

Charley Biggs loves playing tennis and had hopes of becoming a professional player someday. But by the time he got to college, he realized he wasn't going to make it. He pursued a degree in liberal arts because that allowed him to study many subjects. While in college, he spent the summers teaching at tennis camps.

Wall Street was the first stop on his "official" career journey. He spent two years there as a stockbroker, enjoying the work and the pace—for a while.

Then a family friend asked Biggs to work with his new business called U.S. Sports Camps. The idea was to set up top-notch sports camps all over the country in all kinds of sports. It sounded like a winner to Biggs. So he packed his bags and moved across the country to San Francisco to give it a whirl.

He started out at the bottom to the business. Answering phones and registering kids for camps were his primary duties at first. Then he moved up to take charge of a couple of camps. He did a good job and moved up to take charge of an entire sport—basketball at one point and lacrosse at another. He did a little bit of everything to run several camps in several states, including buying equipment and finding

sponsors, locating great facilities, hiring directors, and finding kids to fill the camps! It was like running a business within a business and gave Biggs some great management experience. And, best of all, it gave him a chance to indulge his passion for sports.

TAKE IT TO THE NET

A business like U.S. Sports Camps is made for e-commerce. The same types of people who enrolled in the camps also used computers. The business could reach a national audience with the Internet and could make it easy for people to register for camps on-line.

The business went on-line fairly early in the game, using a basic informational website. Through the years, Biggs and his staff have updated the site with lots of pictures and full descriptions of camps in more than 300 locations. On-line sales have at least doubled each year as they've improved their website.

GOING FOR THE GOAL

U.S. Sports Camps has been a big success, so successful that Biggs has started a new company to apply the same concept to all kinds of camps. Whether it's drama, kayaking, art, or whatever, you'll find a place to enjoy it at Ecamps.com. Find the perfect getaway, register on-line, and you're set for a wild and crazy summer vacation.

THE KID CONNECTION

Looking back, Biggs says he can see some direct connections between what he enjoyed doing as a kid and what he's doing now. There's the sports aspect, of course. But Biggs also says that whenever he wasn't playing tennis, he was reading. He loved to read then and he loves to read now. It helps keep him on top of all the changes in the industry.

Biggs thinks the best thing you can do for your career is to have fun. Find something you enjoy and it will bring out the best in you, giving you the best shot at success.

Entrepreneur

SKILL SET

✔ ADVENTURE

✔ MONEY

✔ WRITING

GO see entrepreneurs in action at any shopping center. Look for bakers, booksellers, specialty shop owners, restaurant owners, and other unique businesses owned by individuals who want to do things their own way.

READ about famous early entrepreneurs such as Henry Ford and C. J. Walker.

TRY finding out your entrepreneurial "IQ" with an on-line assessment at www.ivillage.com/career/quiz.

WHAT IS AN ENTREPRENEUR?

Does the idea of owning your own business appeal to you? If so, you are not alone. According to a Gallup poll, seven out of ten high school students say they want to start their own businesses. Thousands of Americans join the ranks of the self-employed every year. Many of them succeed in ways they never dared to imagine.

An entrepreneur is someone who assumes the risk and responsibility of starting a business. According to the Harvard Business School, an entrepreneur is one who "pursues opportunity beyond the resources currently controlled." In other words, entrepreneurs make something from nothing. They take new ideas, inventions, or products and turn them into profitable enterprises.

Entrepreneurs are just as likely to be found running a business from home as they are working out of an office. Technology such as computers, fax machines, e-mail, and Internet connections has made it possible to run almost any kind of business from almost anywhere. Some entrepreneurs work on their own, using a skill or some special expertise to provide a service or produce a product. Others eventually hire employees to handle specific functions of the business and work together in an office or other type of business establishment. Still other entrepreneurs assemble what are known as "virtual" teams of professionals to provide skills and expertise as needed. These virtual teams are often composed of a variety of self-employed people, often in different places, who share the same entrepreneurial mindset of finding new ways to get the job done.

Essentially, anything that a big company can do, an entrepreneur can do too. The trick is to do it better, faster, or in a new way. Entrepreneurs work in traditional fields such as law, advertising, and accounting as well as cutting-edge industries such as manufacturing, technology, and research. Entrepreneurs produce products that range in complexity from dog toys to computer chips. They provide services that include everything from dry cleaning to health care. Innovation, creativity, and quality are hallmarks of the entrepreneurial approach to business.

In recent years, many of the world's companies have experienced something called "downsizing." That's when a company lays off employees to cut costs. However, since the work still needs to get done, these same companies often contract with entrepreneurs to provide all kinds of services and products. As bad as downsizing often seems, it has provided big opportunities for all kinds of entrepreneurial ventures.

One way to understand the scope of an entrepreneur's work is to remember the story of the little red hen. She was the chick who had a bright idea. She was tired of chicken feed and wanted some delicious bread for a change. Instead of sitting around dreaming about it she got busy planting the wheat, grinding the wheat, mixing the dough, and baking the bread. In the meantime, her pals in the henhouse just went about their regular business. Scratching for chicken feed was fine with them as long as the boss kept it coming. Sure, there were times the little red hen got tired of all that work. After all she had to do *everything*. But in the end, she was the one who got the results: a nice hot loaf of fresh-baked bread. And what did her friends get? More chicken feed!

That's sort of what it's like for entrepreneurs. They come up with the idea for a business, they write the business plan, they dig up the money to start the business (often from their own pockets), they market the product or service, and they make the products or provide the service. In short, they do everything it takes to run the business. If all goes well, they, like the little red hen, eventually get to enjoy the results. In the short run, being an entrepreneur takes a lot more work than an ordinary job. In the long run, it can (but does not always) bring in greater enjoyment and financial results.

Although it can seem hard to believe, entrepreneurs started many of the world's most successful businesses. Ford Motor Company started in the backyard of Henry Ford. Microsoft was started by an unassuming computer geek named Bill Gates (now one of the world's richest computer geeks). Disneyland and all the wonderful animated Disney cartoons began on the drawing board of Walt Disney.

Since the title of "entrepreneur" can be applied to all kinds of small business situations, it probably won't surprise you to learn that there is more than one way to prepare to become an entrepreneur. Increasing numbers of colleges and universities offer "entrepreneurship" training through their business schools. But a successful entrepreneur is just as likely to be someone with a great idea and the courage to make it work as to be someone with a business degree.

However, any business training you get can only be a plus. If you think you might want to start your own business someday, take as many business courses as you can in high school. Get involved in organizations such as Distributive Education Clubs of America (DECA) or cooperative exchange programs that enable you to work in the business world while you attend school. Think about pursuing a college degree in business, marketing, manufacturing, or some area related to your goals. One way or another, you have to know some business basics before you can "go for broke" as an entrepreneur.

Almost without exception, entrepreneurs are risk-takers who are willing to lose it all in order to pursue an idea or business interest that they believe in. They are willing to give up the comfort and security of a nine-to-five job and a regular paycheck in order to work toward something that they see as a bigger and better payoff.

That's why entrepreneurship is not for everyone. Yet for those with that entrepreneurial spirit, it can be an exhilarating and completely satisfying way to make a living. Entrepreneurs bring the innovation and creativity to the marketplace that literally and regularly changes the world—with technology, new and improved products, more efficient services, an energy that never stops trying, and an attitude that doesn't take no for an answer.

TRY IT OUT

NEVER TOO YOUNG

Who says you have to be an adult before you can jump in and try your entrepreneurial skill? Thousands of young people are starting businesses, earning money, and enjoying themselves in the process. Find out how you can join their ranks at these websites just for young entrepreneurs:

Young Entrepreneur's Network at http://www.youngandsuccessful.com is a website run by young entrepreneurs to support the needs of young entrepreneurs from around the world.

YoungBiz at http://www.youngbiz.com is a website "all about the business of being young." It provides a fun and very interactive introduction to the business world, a directory of thousands of young "bizzers," and opportunities to write articles for its newsletter.

Good reads for young entrepreneurs include:

Bernstein, Daryl. *Better Than a Lemonade Stand: Small Business Ideas for Kids.* Hillsboro, Oreg.: Beyond Words Publishing, 1992.

Karnes, Frances A., and Suzanne M. Bean. *Girls and Young Women Inventing: Twenty True Stories About Inventors.* Minneapolis: Free Spirit Publishing, 1995.

Kushell, Jennifer. *The Young Entrepreneur's Edge.* New York: Princeton Review, 1999.

Mariotti, Steve. *The Young Entrepreneurs Guide to Starting and Running a Business.* New York: Times Books, 1996.

ENTREPRENEURS ON-LINE

These websites are geared toward adults but may have some information you can put to use as well.

The Kauffman Center for Entrepreneurial Leadership's website is at http://www.entreworld.org.

National Public Radio keeps a news file on entrepreneurial news at http://www.npr.org/news/business/index_ent.html.

The Edward Lowe Foundation sponsors the Entrepreneurial Edge website at http://edge.lowe.org.

Entrepreneur magazine's on-line 'zine can be found at http://www.entrepreneurmag.com.

CYBER BUSINESS SCHOOL

Starting Your Own Business for Young Entrepreneurs is a free on-line course sponsored by Princeton Review. You can find the course at http://www.hungryminds.com. This course is great and can help give you a jumpstart when and if you actually take that first leap into the world of business. Type in the course name, Starting Your Own Business for Young Entrepreneurs, and the hungry minds search engine will take you directly to the registration page.

MAKE A PLAN

One very important skill you'll learn in the Starting Your Own Business course (described above) is how to make a business plan. Business plans are the road maps entrepreneurs use to turn their ideas into moneymaking ventures.

Create a whizbang plan and take your dreams to the next level by submitting it to the National Business Plan Competition for Teen Women sponsored in part by Charles Schwab, Home Depot, and FleetBoston. Call 1-800-350-1816 to request an application.

Kidsway, Inc., an entrepreneurial education group, sponsors another annual business plan competition (open to both genders). There are special categories for elementary, middle school, and high school students. For more information find the Kidsway website at http://www.kidsway.com or call 1-888-KIDSWAY (that's 1-888-543-7929).

JOIN THE CLUB

Kidsway also sponsors the Young Entrepreneur Club. You have to pay a fee to join, but members get some pretty good stuff: a magazine subscription, book discounts, a club directory, opportunities to network with other young entrepreneurs, and information about entrepreneurial programs. To find out more about the club, visit the Kidsway website at http://www.kidsway.com or call 1-888-KIDSWAY (1-888-543-7929).

SECRETS OF SUCCESS
Learn how some famous entrepreneurs grew their businesses from idea to empire. Some success stories you won't want to miss include:

L. L. Bean, founder of L. L. Bean
Nathan Cummins, creator of Louisville Slugger baseball bats
Walt Disney, founder of all things Disney
John Johnson, magazine publisher
Anita Roddick, founder of The Body Shop
Martha Stewart, founder of Martha Stewart enterprises
David Thomas, founder of Wendy's
Sam Walton, founder of Wal-Mart

To find information, look for books in the library, run searches on the Internet, and keep an eye on the business section of the newspaper for the latest news.

You'll find profiles of famous entrepreneurs in the following books:

Lesonsky, Rieva, and Gayle Sato Stodder. *Young Millionaires: Inspiring Stories to Ignite Your Entrepreneurial Dreams.* Irvine, Calif.: Entrepreneur Media Inc., 1998.

Pile, Robert B. *Top Entrepreneurs and Their Businesses.* Minneapolis: Oliver Press, 1993.

Young, Timothy S., and Richard P. Karlgaard. *Forbes Greatest Technology Stories: Inspiring Tales of the Entrepreneurs and Inventors Who Revolutionized Modern Business.* New York: John Wiley, 1998.

SLEEP ON IT
Summer camps offer unique opportunities to blend fun away from home with learning how to succeed in business. These organizations offer camps with an entrepreneurial angle:

Camp Start Up (offered by Independent Means)
126 Powers Avenue
Santa Barbara, California 93103
800-350-1816
contactus@independentmeans.com
For girls only.

Kidsway, Inc.
5589 Peachtree Street
Chamblee, Georgia 30341
http://www.kidsway.com

You may also want to find out what the following organizations are doing in your town:

Junior Achievement
One Education Way
Colorado Springs, Colorado 80906
http://www.ja.org

4-H Clubs
http://www.4-H.org
This wonderful organization even sponsors "virtual" 4-H clubs online. To join go to http://www.cyfernet.org/virtual4h.

ALL WORK AND NO PLAY?

Play around at learning how to succeed in business with some of the fun resources offered by Independent Means. Browse the aisles of their on-line store at http://www.independentmeans.com for details and ordering instructions for games such as:

Hot Company—The Money Game with Attitude gives you a chance to be the owner of a "hot" new company.

Product in a Box Activity Kit lets you find out what it's like to invent a new product and business.

There's more too. Visit the site and see for yourself.

CHECK IT OUT

The Coleman Foundation
575 West Madison Street, Suite 405
Chicago, Illinois 60661
http://www.colemanfoundation.org

The Consortium for Entrepreneurship Education
601 West Fifth Avenue, PMB 199
Columbus, Ohio 43212
http://www.entre-ed.org

Education, Training, and Enterprise Center
313 Market Street
Camden, New Jersey 08102
http://www.edtecinc.com

Enterprise Ambassador USA
Nova Southeastern University
1750 NE 167th Street
Miami Beach, Florida 33162
http://www.fgse.nova.edu/eausa

The Ewing Marion Kauffman Foundation
4801 Rockhill Road
Kansas City, Missouri 64110
http://www.entreworld.com

The National Coalition for Empowering Youth
    Entrepreneurs
3597 Shannon Drive
Baltimore, Maryland 21213

Youth Venture
3597 North Moore Street, Suite 1920
Arlington, Virginia 22209
http://www.youthventure.org

GET ACQUAINTED

Joline Godfrey, Entrepreneur

CAREER PATH

CHILDHOOD ASPIRATION:
Didn't have a clue about what she wanted to do.

FIRST JOB: Putting milk in the milk cases at her family's dairy.

CURRENT JOB: CEO, Independent Means.

TAKE YOUR PICK

When Joline Godfrey was your age, she somehow got the idea that she, as a woman, had three career options if she didn't want to depend on a husband for support: social worker, librarian, or teacher. She chose social work and used that "traditional" choice as a launching pad to for a successful entrepreneurial venture called Independent Means. Godfrey's business develops products and programs to encourage girls ages 13 to 18 to learn about the world of business and how they can become economically independent. One of the first things that young women learn from Godfrey is that they have choices in life, lots of them.

ONE THING LED TO ANOTHER

Godfrey doesn't consider herself a "born" entrepreneur. She did grow up in a family-owned business watching her grandparents run a small commercial dairy in Maine. While she helped out and learned a lot about what it took to run a business, it never occurred to her that she might one day own one herself. Instead, she says that her career evolved through the years in ways she never imagined. She is the first to admit that there is nothing orderly about her career progression and quickly dismisses the notion of climbing a career "ladder."

After graduating from Boston University with a degree in social work, she joined the corporate ranks working in the affirmative action department at Polaroid, the company famous for inventing instant photography. She describes the time spent at this company as years "marked by unusual opportunity, wonderful mentors, great adventure, and tremendous learning." Perhaps one of the most important lessons she learned at Polaroid came from the company's founder and her personal hero, Dr. Edward Land. Dr. Land was famous for saying that "the only problems worth paying attention to are the impossible ones." Believing that bit of wisdom to be true, Godfrey has based her career on asking tough questions and pursuing the answers.

GIVE IT A TRY—IF YOU DARE

Godfrey advises young people to just start where you are. Let yourself grow and see where it leads you. She says that once you have an idea of what you'd like to do with your life, ask yourself one big question: WHY? The answers you come up with provide important clues about your life's work.

GODFREY: IN WRITING

Get more of Godfrey's ideas in writing by reading some of her books:

No More Frogs to Kiss: 99 Ways to Give Economic Power to Girls. New York: HarperBusiness, 1995.
Our Wildest Dreams: Women Entrepreneurs Making Money, Having Fun, Doing Good. New York: HarperBusiness, 1992.
Twenty Secrets: The Dollar Diva's Guide to Independence. New York: St. Martin's Press, 2000.

To find out more about Godfrey's business, take a look at her website at http://www.dollardiva.com.

Hospitality Manager

SKILL SET

✔ MONEY

✔ TALKING

✔ ADVENTURE

GO visit a really nice restaurant or hotel and see what it's like to provide wonderful service with style.

READ all about various kinds of hospitality careers at http://www.hospitalitycareers.net.

TRY hosting a get-together for some friends. Movie night? A sleepover? What can you do to make sure your guests feel welcome and have a good time?

WHAT IS A HOSPITALITY MANAGER?

Hospitality managers are people who manage hotels, motels, inns, resorts, cruise ships, casinos, or restaurants. They might be responsible for the needs of hundreds of guests on any given night or at any given meal. Hospitality managers could have responsibility for an entire hotel or restaurant or they may be in charge of one department such as catering, the front desk, or housekeeping.

A hospitality manager's main job is to keep the customers happy and coming back for more. That may mean providing "all the comforts of home" for a business traveler or a vacation to remember for a family visiting a resort. One little mix-up can mean the difference between sending guests home smiling or grumbling.

Most hospitality managers find their success in two ways: people and details. A hospitality manager is surrounded by people all day—workers who must be managed and the guests who must be served. So it helps to be a people person. The larger the staff, the more pressure and problems hospitality managers face. They have to make sure that every job gets done even though an employee has called in sick or

quits without notice. Employees have to be trained properly and kept motivated to do a good job. And then there is all that hiring and firing that goes on in an operation like a hotel or restaurant, where employees come and go frequently.

That's the management side of the job. On the hospitality side, there are customers to serve and keep happy. Providing excellent customer service is key to being a successful hospitality manager.

Staying on top of the details is also important to a manager's success. There are many details to deal with every day—some expected and some unexpected. A good hospitality manager can stay cool, calm, and collected no matter what situations occur. Other skills that come in handy for a hospitality manager are communication, organization, and problem solving as well as a solid knowledge of business and finance.

A career in hospitality can take many different forms. There are hospitality management jobs in hotels, on cruise ships, and casinos, and in restaurants. A hospitality management job in the hotel industry alone can include many different positions: the owner/operator of a small bed-and-breakfast, the front desk manager of a national hotel chain like Holiday Inn or Ramada, or the general manager of a fabulous resort on a tropical island.

A hospitality career as an event planner involves coordinating the details for different kinds of events such as corporate meetings, extravagant parties, or weddings. Responsibilities include finding and booking a place to have the event, hiring the best caterer to provide the food, hiring entertainers, and making sure they have all the equipment they need. Event planning can be lots of fun. And an event planner has to be creative so each event has its own special touch. But an event planner also must take responsibility when something goes wrong, and something *always* goes wrong.

Event planners can be part of a hotel or resort staff. They may work for a large corporation that has lots of events, or they can be self-employed and work for all sorts of different clients.

The position of concierge is another interesting hospitality career worth checking out. As part of the hotel staff, the concierge assists guests with making travel arrangements, getting dinner reservations, and obtaining tickets to local attractions. They know their city inside and out so they provide advice about the best places to shop, eat, and sightsee.

Just as there are many different types of hospitality management careers, there are different paths that lead to jobs in the hospitality industry. Hospitality managers used to work their way up through the ranks, starting with a job in housekeeping, at the front desk, or with room service. This still happens, but less often, as preference is given to applicants with a college degree in hotel or restaurant management, marketing, business, or finance. Many universities offer hotel/motel programs. There are also many hospitality vocational programs available that offer specialized training, which can run in length from two weeks to two years. You won't necessarily get a degree but most grant special certification.

A degree doesn't guarantee a cushy management job right out of school. Plan on paying your dues by working in several departments before landing the manager's job. This experience will give you valuable exposure to how different departments operate and will come in handy once you're in charge.

The hospitality industry is huge. If you don't think so, just take a look in the yellow pages under hotels or restaurants. For someone looking for a career with lots of variety and opportunity, hospitality could be just the thing.

TRY IT OUT

MAKE A PLAN

Plan an outing for you and some of your friends. Find something to do that everyone will enjoy and plan all the details. Pick the time and place. Find out how much money each friend will need and arrange the transportation. Invite your friends and make sure they get their parents' permission. A hike in a park? A day at the beach? What about that new amusement park across town? As host of the event, make sure that everyone is having a good time and that everything runs smoothly.

TAKE A TOUR

Contact one of the finer hotels in your area and see if you can arrange a tour. Let the manager know you are exploring hospitality careers and try to see as many of the different departments as possible. Make a list of every hotel job you can think of after you have visited the hotel and rate how interesting you found them.

A DAY IN THE LIFE

See what a day in the life of a hotel general manager and a front desk manager are like and find out about career opportunities at the Drury Hotel's website at http://www.drury-inn.com/lodging/travel/career.htm.

Here are some other sites worth exploring:

☼ Search for careers in the hospitality industry, including hotel, restaurant, casino, resort, and cruise ship jobs, at Hospitality Careers Online at http://www.hcareers.com.

☼ Check out the latest hospitality industry buzz at http://www.hospitalitynet.org.

☼ Visit the Savoy Group's website at http://www.savoygroup. co.uk. There you can visit some of the world's finest hotels, including Claridge's and the Savoy. The Concierge News page may be of special interest if you are interested in that field. The head concierges at four of their properties give some insight into their hospitality experiences.

☼ World Hospitality is an on-line magazine at http://worldhospitality.com that is aimed at helping hotel executives manage all aspects of hotel operations.

☼ Event Planner at http://www.event-planner.com is an Internet resource for event planning. The site has a directory of services event planners need such as caterers, convention centers, party supplies, entertainers, and photographers. You can also keep up-to-date on industry news and employment opportunities.

COME IN AND STAY FOR A WHILE

Visit the library and pick up a few of these books to find out more out careers in hospitality management.

Eberts, Marjorie, Linda Brothers, and Ann Gisler. *Careers in Travel, Tourism, and Hospitality.* Lincolnwood, Ill.: NTC Publishing Group, 1997.

Hawks, John K. *Career Opportunities in Travel and Tourism: A Comprehensive Guide.* New York: Facts On File, 1995.

————. *Travel and Tourism: A Comprehensive Guide to the Exciting Careers Open to You in the Travel and Tourism Industry.* New York: Facts On File, 1996.

Riegel, Carl, and Melissa Dallas. *Hospitality and Tourism Careers: A Blueprint for Success.* New York: Simon & Schuster, 1998.

Rue, Nancy N. *Choosing a Career in Hotels, Motels and Resorts.* New York: Rosen Publishing Group, 1999.

Williams, Anna G., and Karen J. Hall. *Hospitality Skill Sets: Supplement to Your Career Portfolio: At-A-Glance Guide.* Upper Saddle River, N.J.: Prentice-Hall, 1997.

A HAPPENING KIND OF PLACE

Pretend that you've been asked to develop a new resort just for kids your age. You get to start from scratch and do whatever you think will make it great. Get out a notebook and make a plan for the kinds of food you'll serve, the kinds of activities you'll offer, what the guest rooms will look like, and so on. If you really want to go crazy, make sketches of the layout of your resort. Or clip pictures from magazines that have the look of your ultimate vacation spot.

CHECK IT OUT

The American Hotel & Motel Association
1201 New York Avenue NW, Suite 600
Washington, D.C. 20005
http://www.ahma.com

Council on Hotel, Restaurant, and Institutional Education
1200 17th Street NW
Washington, D.C. 20036

Hotel Sales and Marketing Association International
1300 L Street, NW, Suite 1020
Washington, D.C. 20005

Meeting Professionals International
4455 LBJ Freeway, Suite 1200

Dallas, Tex. 75244-5903
http://www.mpiweb.org

National Concierge Association
P.O. Box 2860
Chicago, Ill. 60690-2860
http://www.conciergeassoc.org

National Executive Housekeepers Association, Inc.
1001 Eastwind Drive, Suite 301
Westerville, Ohio 43081

National Restaurant Association Educational Foundation
250 Wacker Street, Suite 1400
Chicago, Ill. 60606-5834
http://www.restaurant.com

GET ACQUAINTED

Sylvia Varney,
Hospitality Manager

CAREER PATH

CHILDHOOD ASPIRATION: To be a lawyer.

FIRST JOB: Waitress at a Chinese restaurant.

CURRENT JOB: Co-owner, Fredericksburg Herb Farm.

THE VERDICT IS IN

From the time she was a young girl, Sylvia Varney wanted to become a lawyer. She was addicted to *Perry Mason* (a television show about a lawyer) and wanted to get a job where she could advise, protect, and support the downtrodden. She wanted to be a lawyer so badly that she was halfway through law school before she realized it was the wrong career for her. In all her plans she'd forgotten to ask herself the all-important question: why?

Yes, she wanted to help people but she was uncomfortable working in the gray areas that lawyers often encounter. She is a big believer in right and wrong and didn't like having to set that aside to represent clients. Unable to find the emotional detachment so necessary when working with people in serious crisis, she just didn't think she could handle making the tough decisions lawyers often have to make.

Varney discovered this problem before it was too late to do something about it. She transferred over to the business school and went after a master's in business administration. There she found her talents put to better use. She learned to develop an idea and take it to market as a finished product that people want to buy.

AN IDEA TAKES ROOT

In 1985, Varney and her husband, Bill, decided to leave the corporate fast track and start their own business. They weren't even sure what the business would be and took some time trying to find just the right opportunity in their delightful Texas town. They eventually decided that a shop offering luxury bath and body products was just what the town needed.

They opened the shop selling wonderful products made by other companies. However, behind the shop there was a small garden that Mr. Varney just couldn't resist. Before long, the Varney's were growing lavender, rosemary, and herbs. Needing something to do with the bounty of their garden, Sylvia Varney started learning all she could about herbs. Next she started sharing her newfound knowledge by offering classes about herbs and creating all kinds of new products with herbs. Herbal vinegars, potpourri, sachets, and teas were among the products that were soon flying out of her shop.

A GROWING SUCCESS

Today the business has grown into a million-dollar business with customers all over the world. It includes several acres of gardens, a mail-order catalog, two shops at the farm, another shop in town, a day spa where guests are pampered with facials and massages, a restaurant where guests are treated to an enticing array of food gussied up with herbs (how about a pesto turkey wrap or some cheddar and chive tomato pie?), and a bed-and-breakfast inn. Talk about hospitality! People come to Varney's farm for the peaceful, healing experience that all Varney's extra efforts help create.

ANGELS ON HER SIDE

Varney says that there have been lots of "angels" who have helped make the business what it is today. Some of those angels are among the 30 employees who work for the farm and truly believe in what they are doing, and some of those angels are the people who keep buying and enjoying the products. She also credits her faith for carrying her through the "roller coaster" times that come with owning such a multifaceted operation.

International Trade Specialist

SHORTCUTS

GO host a foreign exchange student or become one yourself when you get old enough. But get your parents' permission first!

READ everything you can find about other places and peoples. Keep up with current events to learn about history in the making.

TRY eating out at a restaurant that specializes in food from another country such as Thailand, Vietnam, or Ireland.

WHAT IS AN INTERNATIONAL TRADE SPECIALIST?

Traveling the globe in search of exotic products to sell at home can be one of the glamorous perks of being an international trade specialist. An international trade specialist is either an importer (someone who brings products into a country) or an exporter (someone who sells products in other countries) or both. The United States trades goods with countries all over the world. Some of the biggest U.S. trading partners are Canada, Japan, Germany, the United Kingdom, France, and Mexico.

Exporting any type of product involves handling lots of details. Researching potential markets, making contact with companies in foreign countries who will sell their products, dealing with foreign governments, and preparing goods to be shipped overseas are typical parts of a day's work for an international trade specialist. Dealing with customs and all the rules and regulations in each country is another big part of this job.

International Trade Specialist

Importers also deal with foreign governments, customs, and shipping. Their job is to identify products that are likely to be a big hit in their home country. Then they negotiate good prices and make efforts to get the products to their country. They often take "shopping" trips to different countries in search of special items that other people will want to buy. Good taste and an eye for what sells are important for an importer.

Sometimes international trade specialists work for major corporations such as Coca-Cola, Nike, and IBM. Companies like these export their products to foreign markets and hire international trade specialists to get the job done. They may also import various materials or depend on international partners to provide labor to produce certain products.

Other international trade specialists are self-employed businesspeople who either sell products to other countries or import goods to sell in their countries. They may own a specialty shop (or shops) and scour the world for special products to sell, or they may specialize in a certain type of product such as jewelry or exotic foods that they provide to other clients. Sometimes these entrepreneurs have a background in international trade, and sometimes they just come across a great product or have the "perfect" idea and decide to make a go of it. Either way, there's lots to learn. Training such as that offered by the U.S. Department of Commerce's International Trade Administration often means the difference between growing a business or failing. Good communication skills are a must for an international trade specialist, and fluency in more than one language, while not an absolute requirement, is helpful. International trade specialists must be knowledgeable about the legal requirements of their home countries as well as the other countries they are dealing with. Some international trade specialists have a legal background, which can prove extremely useful.

A good international trade specialist has to be a problem solver too. Things do not always go smoothly when products are being shipped thousands of miles away and foreign governments are involved. Oceans, equipment, language barriers, current events, and all kinds of obstacles can conspire to wreak havoc on even the best-laid plans. When things go badly, diplomacy is the key to sorting things out.

Some international trade specialists actually live in foreign countries. Such experience can be beneficial for people who are flexible and willing to adapt to local conditions and customs. They must keep up on political and economic conditions that might affect their ability to do business.

Several different paths can lead you to a career in world trade. Many universities offer undergraduate degrees and master's programs in international business. These programs often include specialties in different regions of the world and intense foreign language study as well as international business courses in which students learn the details of doing business in other countries. Some require that you work in a foreign country for six months as an intern. This valuable experience can give you a foot in the door when you are looking for that first job.

To increase your chances of landing a job in international trade, get a college degree in business, law, or accounting, and don't forget the foreign language. Also, seriously consider an advanced degree in international business.

Another way to add an international flair to your career path is to become a foreign exchange trader. This isn't a field you jump into without specialized training, but it can be rewarding and financially lucrative as well. A foreign exchange trader basically trades currency or money between different countries. It probably sounds easier than it is. This is an exciting but risky career as just one transaction can involve millions of dollars! Foreign exchange traders often have degrees in economics, mathematics, or statistics. It's a field to look into if a finance-related career in international business sounds interesting to you.

All in all, a career in international trade can offer plenty of travel and adventure. But it also requires lots of hard work and business skills to get those products where they need to go.

TRY IT OUT

TALK THE TALK

Take a trip to your local or on-line computer store (with your parents' permission, of course) and search out some software that will help you learn a foreign language. There are several programs available and some are very inexpensive. Berlitz offers a Think and Talk series in Italian, Spanish, French, or German. These products are published by The Learning Company in Boston and can be ordered on-line at http://www.learningco.com. Work through a language or two and discover if you like talking in another language.

Another fun way to build your international vocabulary is at the Traveling Word of the Day website at http://www.travlang.com/wordofday. Each day you can hear a new word or phrase translated into 50 different languages.

GO SHOPPING!

Next time you hit the mall, visit a gift shop and note where the different goods were made. This will give you a feel for the kinds of products that are imported and where they come from. Make a list of countries and keep track of the types of products you find. Can you tell a difference in the quality of products manufactured in different countries?

GLOBE-TROTTING WITH THE CIA

Visit the CIA's World Factbook website at www.odci.gov/cia/publications/factbook/index.html. Here you'll find tons of "intelligence" information about every country in the world. It has detailed information about each country's geography, population, government, and economy, including what kind of products they import and export and what countries they do business with. Check out several countries that seem interesting to you and find out what they are trading.

HIT THE ZONE

The ExportZone U.S.A. website at www.exportzone.com contains links to hundreds of sites. It will tell you everything you ever wanted to know about international trade and more. You will find links to foreign countries, sites that convert currency, on-line trade publications, and places to go for assistance.

While you're on-line, visit the American Export Register at www.aernet.com. This site has listings for more than 45,000 companies that export in 5,000 different product categories. Try searching for something unusual like pet food and see what you come up with.

Other websites with an international flair include:

- World Trade Organization at http://www.wto.org/
- Doing Business Abroad at http://www.hg.org/guides.html
- Entrepreneur International at http://www.entrepreneurmag.com/international/hts
- World Trade Zone at http://www.worldtradezone.com
- Global Business Web at http://www.globalbusinessweb.com
- Currency Converter at http://www.oanda.com/cgi%2Dbin/ncc
- Serra International at http://www.serraintl.com
- Trade Compass at http://www.tradecompass.com

AN ARMCHAIR ADVENTURE

See the world from the comfort of your favorite spot at home. Gather up a bunch of travel guides from the library and get a glimpse of some of the exotic places you could someday work in. For ideas about things you could do to earn a living, try thumbing through books such as these:

Bell, Arthur. *Great Jobs Abroad.* New York: McGraw-Hill, 1999.

Knappman, Edward W. *American Jobs Abroad.* New York: Gale Research, 1994.

Kocher, Eric, and Nina Segal. *International Jobs: Where They Are and How to Get Them.* Cambridge, Mass.: Perseus Books, 1998.

Krannich, Ronald, and Caryl Rae Krannich. *The Complete Guide to International Jobs and Careers.* Manassas, Va.: Impact Publications, 1998.

———. *International Jobs Directory.* Manassas, Va.: Impact Publications, 1998.

Sautters, Joyce. *The Adventure of Working Abroad: Hero Tales from the Global Frontier.* San Francisco: Jossey-Bass, 1995.

CHECK IT OUT

Federation of International Trade Associations
11800 Sunrise Valley Drive, Suite 210
Reston, Virginia 20191
(800) 969-3482
http://www.fita.org

International Small Business Consortium
2015 Martingale Drive
Norman, Oklahoma 73072
http://www.isbc.com

International Trade Association
1244 North Nokomis NE
Alexandria, Minnesota 56308
(320) 763-5101
http://www.expertpages.com/org/ita.htm

GET ACQUAINTED

Susan Gravely,
International Trade Specialist

CAREER PATH

CHILDHOOD ASPIRATION: To be the wife of an ambassador.

FIRST JOB: Wrapping presents in an upscale clothing store.

CURRENT JOB: President of Vietri, an Italian dinnerware and accessories import company.

READY FOR ANYTHING

When Susan Gravely was a young girl, her favorite movie was *Gone With the Wind*. She admits it sounds kind of weird, but her favorite character was Mammy, the family's maid. Gravely recognized that Mammy was a really good person who got a lot done, and she wanted to grow up to be just like her.

She also remembers finding her father's work in international business fascinating. She loved entertaining people from all over the world in their home. She discovered if she volunteered to help serve the drinks, she could sit in on all the interesting conversations.

But Gravely was raised during a time when society didn't have many career expectations for women. The general idea was for women to marry successful men and let them take care of earning the money. Even so, Gravely always had a feeling that she wanted to provide for herself.

And, in a way, her life prepared her for success on her own by teaching her how to work hard. Whether it was running a lemonade stand, baby-sitting, or volunteering with her church group, Gravely was always busy doing something. Even as a Girl Scout, she enjoyed working toward new badges.

A HOLIDAY TO REMEMBER

Although Gravely never intended to become president of a wildly successful company, there are some common themes in her work that brought her to this place. Color, people, and building things have made frequent appearances in many of the job choices she's made along the way.

After college, she took a job with an architectural firm. Then she started designing play spaces for sick children at hospitals and doctors' offices. Then she helped a friend open three retail stores. But things started really coming together when she took a nine-month sabbatical to study interior design in New York City.

It was at this point that her mother invited Gravely and her sister on a trip to Italy's Amalfi coast. It was there that the women fell in love—with dinnerware. With nothing to lose (except, of course, their $20,000 investment), they decided to start a business importing Italian dishes. Talk about being in the right place at the right time!

Their company's product line started with some colorful and elegant dishes they traced to a factory in Vietri (hence the name of their company), and it has grown to include tableware and glassware from 40 Italian manufacturers. From the northern part of Italy, they find products made from white clay, called terra bianca, which are decorated with fruit, flowers, animals, and fish. Southern Italy offers up a dazzling array of products made from red clay, called terra-cotta. These dishes are often brightly glazed in cool yellows and blues. Some of the designs have been used since the 1300s and have been handed down from generation to generation.

Through the years, Vietri has grown to employ 42 people in its main office and 60 sales representatives. More than 3,500 better gift stores and retail stores in the United States carry Vietri's products.

As president of the company, Gravely makes about four trips to Italy every year to meet with manufacturers and designers. She also visits places such as France and Germany for inspiration. Gravely considers the travel to be one of the best parts of running an international business. She appreciates the real friendships she has found in working with the Italian merchants and artisans.

A SIMPLE PLAN

At this point, Gravely has realized that you can't make everything happen in your life. There's only so much you actually *do*, so that's why making good choices is so important. Gravely has decided that the best thing she can do now is enjoy her family and work hard.

Gravely says that success seems to follow when her focus is on making her business the best it can be. Loving her work, keeping the right balance between work and her family responsibilities, and finding free time to enjoy the people and projects she most cares about—now that's Gravely's idea of a *bellissimo* (beautiful) life.

Investment Banker

SKILL SET

✔ MATH
✔ MONEY
✔ TALKING

WHAT IS AN INVESTMENT BANKER?

Investment bankers help companies and governments issue securities, and they help investors purchase securities, manage financial assets, trade securities, and provide financial advice. Working in investment banking is often a lot like riding on a roller coaster. It can be a high-powered business environment with deals involving millions and even billions of dollars.

If you decide to go into investment banking, you will probably end up working in one of four areas: corporate finance, sales, trading, or research. Here's a brief rundown on what each area involves.

Bankers working in corporate finance provide financial consulting to businesses. They help clients come up with sound financial strategies and give advice on complex business dealings such as mergers and acquisitions (buying or taking over other businesses), foreign exchange, and economic and market trends.

The sales area involves selling new debt and equity issues generated by the corporate finance area of the house. For instance, a bank might issue a number of 30-year mortgage loans to individuals and then turn around and sell this debt to another bank or lending institution in order to get a quicker payoff. It's a technical area that most banks only entrust to experienced bankers or those who have already earned MBAs.

The trading area is tougher, riskier, and more intense than any other type of financial job. It involves working with stocks and securities, and it requires dealing with the stock market.

The research area is where some of the most influential bankers in the business work. These people research market and economic trends, analyze what they learn, and make predictions about "hot" stocks and investment opportunities. Their ongoing success is determined by how accurate their predictions are.

No matter what area they work in, investment bankers must be comfortable with numbers. Spreadsheets and complex mathematical equations are part and parcel of the job. Investment bankers become expert in calculating what a business is worth.

The best positions in investment banking go to those with advanced degrees such as an MBA (master's in business administration), a CMA (certified management accountant), or CFA (certified financial analyst). This means that, at the very least, you'll need a college degree in business, economics,

or some other related subject just to get your foot in the door. And that will carry you just so far. An advanced degree is usually required for advancement in this field.

If you are thinking about a career in this field, keep in mind that the biggest players in investment banking are located near the financial center of the country: Wall Street in New York City. Other investment banking hotbeds include London, San Francisco, and Silicon Valley. There are also international opportunities for bankers working in Frankfurt, Tokyo, Hong Kong, and other foreign markets. There are investment banks in other parts of the world, of course, but these places are usually home to the biggest deals. If you want to be where the action is, you may have to pack your bags to get there.

Earnings in investment banking can be high. In some cases, investment bankers start bringing in six-figure salaries within a couple of years on the job. However, the work can be stressful, requiring long hours and dealing with some pretty intense people. There is both risk and reward in this profession, so you really have to weigh the pros and cons to decide if this is the career for you.

TRY IT OUT

BIG-TIME BANKING
Goldman Sachs, Merrill Lynch, and Morgan Stanley are three of the biggest names in the investment banking business. Visit their websites and see what you can learn about the types of services these banks offer.

- ☼ Goldman Sachs at http://www.gs.com
- ☼ Merrill Lynch at http://www.ml.com
- ☼ Morgan Stanley Dean Witter at http://www.msdw.com

Compare them and pick which one you'd choose to work with if you had a cool million to invest.

WHO WANTS TO BE A MILLIONAIRE?

You don't have to answer questions on a game show to make your millions. Visit the Invest Smart website and find out how the power of compounding interest can make you a millionaire by investing only $100 a month. You'll find lots of other fun ways to learn your way around investment banking at http://www.library.thinkquest.org/10326/market_simulation/mutual.html.

Another website especially for kids is http://www.younginvestor.com. Here you'll find a game room, a library, and even stuff for your parents.

BANKING ON A CAREER IN BANKING

Read some of the following books to broaden your horizons about opportunities in the world of finance.

Alpert, Gary. *So You Want to be an Investment Banker?* San Francisco: WetFeet, 2000.

Liaw, K. Thomas. *The Business of Investment Banking.* New York: John Wiley, 1999.

Naficy, Mariam. *The Fast Track: The Insider's Guide to Winning Jobs in Management Consulting, Investment Banking, and Securities Trading.* New York: Broadway Books, 1997.

Pandey, Aril, and Omotayo T. Okusanya. *Harvard Business School Career Guide: Finance.* Boston: Harvard Business School Press, 2000.

Robinson, Mark. *Business and Finance Career Directory.* Detroit: Gale Research, 1993.

PRACTICE WHAT YOU PREACH

If you ever hope to have other people trust you with their millions, learn to manage your own money now. Here are a few resources to help you get started:

Berg, Adriene C. *The Totally Awesome Money Book for Kids.* New York: Newmarket Press, 1993.

Godfrey, Neale S. *Money Doesn't Grow on Trees*. New York: Simon and Schuster, 1998.

Otfinoski, Steve. *The Kid's Guide to Money: Earning It, Saving It, Spending It, Growing It, Sharing It*. New York: Scholastic, 1996.

CHECK IT OUT

American Association of Individual Investors
625 North Michigan Avenue
Chicago, Illinois 60611
http://www.aaii.com

American Bankers Association
1120 Connecticut Avenue NW
Washington, D.C. 20036
http://www.aba.com

American Financial Services Association
919 18th Street, Suite 300
Washington, D.C. 20006
http://www.afsaef.org

Association of Investment Management and Research
P.O. Box 3668
Charlottesville, Virginia 22901
http://www.aimr.com

Institute of Financial Education
55 West Monroe, Suite 2800
Chicago, Illinois 60603
http://www.theinstitute.com

National Association of Investors Corporation
P.O. Box 220
Royal Oak, Michigan 48068
http://www.better-investing.org

National Center for Financial Education
P.O. Box 34070
San Diego, California 92163-4070
http://www.ncfe.org

GET ACQUAINTED

Joann Price,
Investment Banker

CAREER PATH

CHILDHOOD ASPIRATION: To work in a library.

FIRST JOB: Shelving books in a library.

CURRENT JOB: Vice president, Young Americans Bank.

BOOKS TO BANKING

As a child, Joann Price enjoyed nothing quite as much as a good book. To this day, she loves hanging around libraries and bookstores. She even went to college to prepare for a career as a librarian.

But life took a different turn when, after graduating from college, she moved to a small Colorado mountain town with her husband. Jobs were few and far between. No positions were available at the local library, but the local community bank needed someone to work at the accounts desk. In fact, they need someone so badly that they asked her start right after the interview!

Working at a small-town bank turned out to be a good start for Price's unexpected career in banking. It was easier to move ahead, and Price was able to work her way up from the accounts desk, to supervisor, to retail bank manager, and eventually vice president. It proved to be an ideal setting for an on-the-job education in banking.

BIG-CITY BANKING

When Price and her family relocated to Denver, she continued working in banking. She gained experience by working for a bank and trust. She started working in what is known as "relationship banking," handling all the banking needs of specific clients. She worked, in particular, with clients in real estate and oil and gas businesses.

Next came stints in executive banking and private banking. Then she worked with the FDIC (Federal Deposit Insurance Corporation) during the 1980s, an era when the savings and loan industry was in serious financial crisis. While she was with it the FDIC closed hundreds of banks and savings and loan institutions.

PINT-SIZED BANKING

Now Price is vice president of the Young Americans Bank, one of the most unusual banks in the world. It's a bank just for kids and is a project of the Young Americans Education Foundation. Clients are between the ages of birth to 22 years. The bank handles about 16,000 accounts with an average balance of $400. It offers all the same kinds of service that an "adult" bank offers—including savings accounts and checking accounts—and even issues credit cards (with a $100 limit) and offers loans to clients with a valid plan and the means to repay it. The biggest difference between the Young Americans Bank and a regular bank is education: the Young Americans Bank offers all kinds of learning programs to help its young clients become financially savvy.

One of the bank's most exciting programs is called Young Ameritowne, in which kids learn how to handle money in the context of a kid-sized "town." Kids apply for jobs doing things like running the town bank, the daily newspaper, the soda shop, and the print shop. There's a mayor and a hospital too. Kids get a paycheck and a checkbook, and they use the cash to buy the things they want and need to live in Young Ameritowne. It's an unforgettable way to learn about money.

THE CHILDREN'S BANKER

As vice president of the bank, Price is responsible for the day-to-day operations of the bank. One of her favorite parts of the job is working with her young clients. It's a return to the "relationship" banking concept since she works individually with clients to help them figure out their financial goals and help them understand what it will take to reach them. If you were to visit her, she would help you make a plan by asking you questions such as:

- What are you saving for?
- How much money do you need?
- How much money can you save?
- When will you need it?

If you were interested in investing in stocks or a mutual fund, she would make sure that you understood that it wasn't a way to get rich quick. You've got to be prepared to win or lose. Investing is just one part of your financial plan. If you are careful, it is something that can be a lot of fun. Price advises her young clients to invest in companies that they like.

ON-LINE BANKING

You can find out more about the Young Americans Bank by visiting its website at http://www.theyoungamericans.org.

Lawyer

SHORTCUTS

SKILL SET

✔ TALKING

✔ WRITING

✔ MONEY

GO spend a day watching lawyers in action at the local courthouse.

READ all kinds of mysteries to try your luck at "cracking the case."

TRY watching reruns of *Perry Mason, Matlock,* and *Law and Order* on television to get a semirealistic look at what it's like to be an attorney.

WHAT IS A LAWYER?

The main thing that any type of lawyer does is to advise people or businesses about legal matters and to act as their advocate in legal affairs. Most lawyers (also known as attorneys) specialize in either criminal or civil law. There are two sides to criminal law: the defense and the prosecution. Defense attorneys represent someone who is accused of a crime in trial proceedings. Prosecutors, often working through a state or federal district attorney's office, represent the "people" in bringing charges against a suspected criminal. You've probably seen shows on televisions that depict how these two sides of the legal system work.

On the civil side, a lawyer may specialize in a certain kind of law such as family law, real estate, tax law, trusts, wills, and other legal matters. A particularly hot area for civil attorneys is corporate law. These types of lawyers may specialize in a wide range of business issues, including corporate financing, contracts, acquisitions, bankruptcy, and employee benefits. The objective is to get deals done legally so that problems don't come up in the future.

The other kind of corporate law deals with the problems that do come up. These kinds of attorneys are often called litigators, and they represent corporate clients who are dealing

with potential problems such as breaches of contract, class-action lawsuits, and white-collar crime.

For better or worse, lawsuits have become more common in our society. As if crime alone couldn't account for enough legal activity, law now plays a part in virtually every part of business and, in many ways, life in general. For example, if someone slips on the ice in front of your house, they may have grounds to sue you. Big areas of growth in legal action involve areas such as employee benefits, health care, intellectual property, sexual harassment, the environment, and real estate.

If you watch any law shows on TV, you may get the idea that lawyers spend most of their time at court, arguing cases before a judge and jury. Not so. Even if their work does involve court appearances, and some lawyers rarely even step inside a courtroom, most lawyers' time is spent in a law library doing research or sitting behind a computer writing contracts, briefs, and other types of legal documentation. All this homework can make the difference between winning or losing a case.

One of the biggest challenges a potential lawyer faces is getting into law school. Since there are so many applications

from aspiring lawyers, law schools can be particular about who they pick. Good (make that excellent) grades in college are vital. There is no absolute "prelaw" major but many law students find a background in political science, government, history, economics, or business to be helpful. What's important is a major that provides plenty of opportunity to hone skills in writing, reading, thinking logically, and communicating effectively. Law school applicants must also pass the LSAT (law school admission test).

For those lucky enough to make it into law school and to successfully complete three years of study there, the next big hurdle is passing the bar exam. Each state issues its own version of this really tough, six-hour-long test. The exam is so challenging that many students take special classes just to prepare for it, study for months, and still end up having to take it more than once before they pass.

When it's time to find a job, most lawyers either open their own private practice or join a law firm. Others find jobs either with a local government or in federal agencies such as the Department of Justice, the Treasury Department, or the Department of Defense. The rest are employed as house counsel by business firms, religious groups, or nonprofit organizations.

If the pursuit of justice is something you care about and you think you're ready to handle some tough questions, consider law as a career in which you can make a difference.

TRY IT OUT

GET YOUR FEET WET
To find all kinds of interesting information about the legal profession, be sure to visit http://www.wetfeet.com. Click on the career advice icon and type in "lawyer." You'll find all kinds of links and resources that can help guide your career decision. Other law-related websites that you can look at include:

🔆 http://www.findlaw.com (there's a special section for students that you might like to see)

🔆 http://www.lawyers.com (where you can find information about a wide variety of legal issues)

🔆 http://www.lawoffice.com (a place to look for information about more than 400 legal topics)

🔆 http://www.lawguru.com (a site where people go to find free answers to more than 7,000 legal questions)

See what you can find out about students' rights at some of these sites.

EASY LEGALESE

Like any profession, law comes with its own vocabulary, sometimes known as "legalese." Visit wetfeet.com's legal lingo glossary at http://www.wetfeet.com/industries/law/glossary. asp to find out what some of the following terms mean:

🔆 Act of God
🔆 Arraignment
🔆 Brief
🔆 Cop a plea
🔆 Due process
🔆 Good Samaritan law
🔆 Hung jury
🔆 Pro bono
🔆 Quid pro quo
🔆 Take the fifth

WHO'S WHO IN LAW

Law firms come in all shapes and sizes. Some are private practices run by just one attorney, while others are major firms employing thousands of lawyers in offices all over the world. Following are web addresses for some of the biggest firms around. Visit their websites to get a feel for what their specialties might be.

☼ Baker & McKenzie at http://www.bakerinfo.com
☼ Davis, Polk & Wardwell at http://www.dpw.com
☼ Jones, Day, Reavis & Pogue at http://www.jonesday.com
☼ Latham & Watkins at http://www.lw.com
☼ Mayer, Brown & Platt at http://www.mayerbrown.com
☼ Shearman & Sterling at http://www.shearman.com
☼ Sidley & Austin at http://www.sidley.com
☼ Skadden, Arps, Slate, Meagher & Flom at http://www.sasmf.com
☼ Sullivan & Cromwell at http://www.sullcrom.com

What kinds of clients are they likely to serve? Do you think you'd like to work for a firm like one of these? Why or why not?

THROW THE BOOK AT YOUR CAREER

Here are some books that can give you more ideas about a lawful future:

Law School Admission Council. *So You Want to be a Lawyer.* New York: Broadway Books, 1998.

Lee, Mary Price. *100 Best Careers in Crime Fighting: Law Enforcement, Criminal Justice, Private Security, and Cyberspace Crime Detection.* New York: IDG Books Worldwide, 1997.

Mantis, Hillary. *Alternative Careers for Lawyers.* New York: Princeton Review, 1997.

Munneke, Gary A. *Careers In Law.* Lincolnwood, Ill.: VGM Career Horizons, 1997.

Turnicky, Ann. *How to Get the Job You Want in a Law Firm.* New York: John Wiley, 1997.

Walton, Kimm Alayne. *Guerrilla Tactics for Getting the Legal Job You Want.* New York: Harcourt Brace, 1997.

YOU BE THE JUDGE

For a fascinating—and fun—look at a streamlined version of the court system in the real world, visit icourthouse.com. Here you can be a juror, view the evidence, and present your case on-line. And the verdict is . . .

CHECK IT OUT

American Bar Association
541 North Fairbanks Court
Chicago, Illinois 60611-3314
http://www.abanet.org

American Corporate Council Association
1025 Connecticut Avenue NW, Suite 200
Washington, D.C. 20036
http://www.acca.com

Association of Trial Lawyers of America
1050 31st Street NW
Washington, D.C. 20007
http://www.atlahq.org

GET ACQUAINTED

Cynthia Tucker, Attorney

CAREER PATH

CHILDHOOD ASPIRATION:
Toyed with different ideas at different times. Thought about being a teacher and considered trying to fulfill her mother's dream of singing on Broadway but reconsidered when she realized that she couldn't sing!

FIRST JOB: Flight attendant for international airlines.

CURRENT JOB: Attorney with her own general law practice.

A FAMILY AFFAIR

Cynthia Tucker grew up in a family of seven children. Her father was the first black bus driver in her hometown of Springfield, Massachusetts. Tucker was just 12 years old when her dad died, leaving her mom to raise and support the family on her own. Tucker is still not sure how her mom managed to do that and put all seven children through college on her earnings from running a beauty salon in their home. Tucker remembers that her mother worked from sunup to sundown and always wanted a better life for her children. Today three of the seven kids are lawyers, one of them is a doctor, one is an educational counselor, and the other two are in business.

AROUND THE WORLD AND BACK

Law wasn't Tucker's first choice for a career. In college, she majored in sociology and assumed she'd pursue a career in social work. A couple of unrelated circumstances changed everything for her. Tucker's first experience with the law came through some work she did with the American Civil Liberties Union on a project that examined the hiring practices at local television stations. Although her participation was strictly from a sociological standpoint, she was intrigued with the legal aspects of the project.

Her second exposure to legal ideas came about after college when she went to work as an international flight attendant. While traveling around the world, Tucker became fascinated with international law and treaties. She also discovered that she got airsick a lot, which made working as a flight attendant not such a good career choice for her.

FLYING IN A NEW DIRECTION

Next stop for Tucker's career was law school, which she describes as a "relentless" experience in learning. It takes a lot of reading and research to cultivate a legal mind, and Tucker worked hard to complete the program—even after marrying and having a child.

If law school was tough, passing the bar exam proved even tougher. Tucker didn't pass it the first time, but she was determined to get it right no matter what. Keeping an eye on her goal and maintaining her focus, Tucker's perseverance paid off after taking the bar exam several times.

While pursuing acceptance by the bar, Tucker worked as a legislative aide for a state senator. The work involved drafting new legislation and was something Tucker enjoyed for several years.

SETTING UP SHOP

Several years ago, Tucker went out on her own and established her own general practice law firm. General practice means that Tucker does a little bit of everything. Family law, real estate, and personal injury are areas that keep her busy, and she has to keep up with frequently changing laws.

Whatever the situation, be it a divorce or an accident involving an injury, Tucker's goal as an attorney is always to reach a compromise that makes sense for everyone involved. Winning isn't as important as doing the right thing.

Life as an attorney isn't nearly as glamorous and exciting as TV law shows sometimes make it appear. There is a lot of behind-the-scenes research and preparation in each case. And, believe it or not, Tucker tries to avoid the courtroom as much as possible. Instead, she works to settle most cases through common sense and keen negotiation skills.

THE ROAD TO SUCCESS

Success will come, says Tucker, when someone enjoys his or her work, stays motivated, and finds passion in what he or she is doing. She advises young people to "be involved and be actively patient" in whatever it is that interests them. You can't just sit around waiting for success to come your way. Stay active, and change will come.

Management Consultant

SHORTCUTS

GO to Disneyland or Disney World to see one of the world's most respected companies in action.

READ Chad Foster's book, *Teenagers: Preparing for the Real World* (Lithonia, Ga.: Rising Books, 1995).

TRY offering good advice to a friend with a problem.

SKILL SET

✔ MONEY
✔ TALKING
✔ WRITING

WHAT IS A MANAGEMENT CONSULTANT?

What does a small company that needs better control over its expenses have in common with a huge manufacturing company looking to relocate to another state? Both companies could benefit from a management consultant. Management consultants help businesses solve all kinds of problems—some simple, some very complex. Since most businesses like the idea of being more efficient and more profitable, there is a huge market for the services of management consultants.

Probably the best way to get into management consulting is by working for a consulting company. Consulting firms range in size from just one consultant to large international companies that employ thousands of consultants. These firms tend to be the largest employees of the top MBAs (master's in business administration) and college graduates. The pay is good, the opportunities are plentiful, and it's the kind of career that can take you places—all over the world, in some cases.

No matter the size of the companies they work with, all consultants must have a special kind of expertise that other companies will pay to get. It may be legal expertise, accounting expertise, or very specialized expertise in businesses such as the health care industry or information technology. Hot areas in the consulting field include e-business consulting, creating competitive work environments, and branding (strategies to get customers to recognize a particular product or company). The one thing that all consulting firms have in common is smart people. The only product they have to sell is their consultants' advice, so it had better be good.

Management consultants must be good at conducting research and analyzing what it means. Research might involve interviewing employees, collecting information from the client or related organizations, and conducting surveys and market studies. The ideas is to discover trends or factors that negatively affect a client's success and determine ways to turn things around.

Seasoned consultants often go into business for themselves with varying degrees of success. It's a popular career choice for business experts because it's a relatively inexpensive business to start. Since the product they sell is their own expertise, they don't have to pay for fancy equipment and materials. Of course, management consultants will succeed only if they have the expertise that other businesses need and will pay to get.

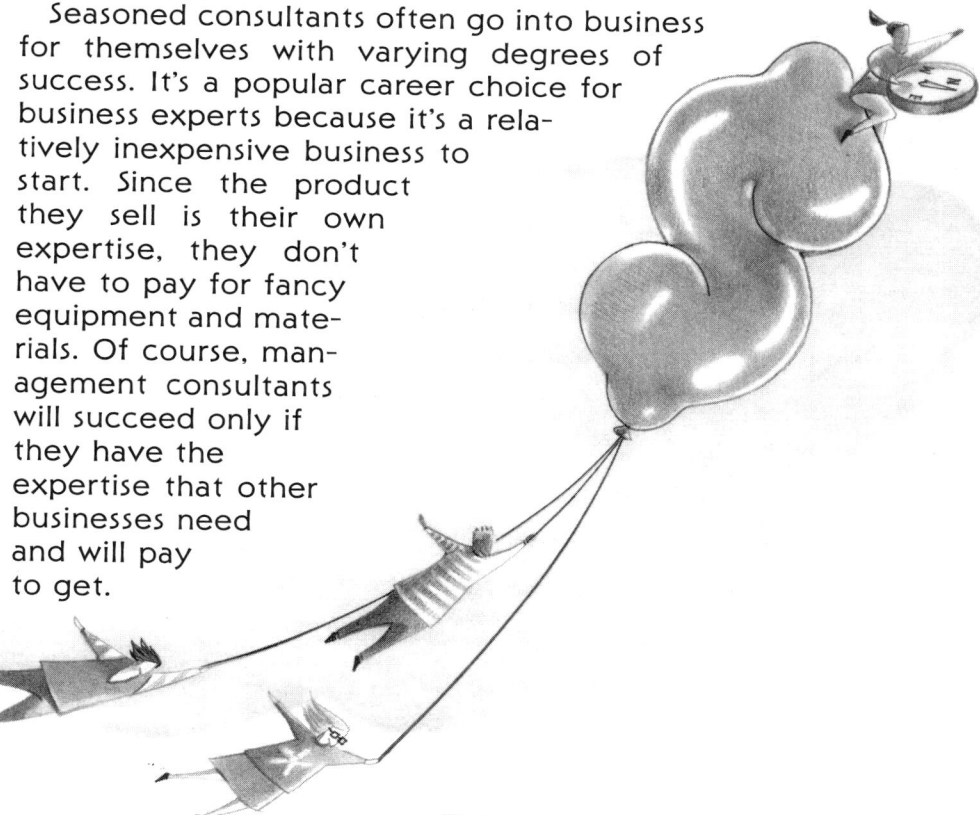

What do you have to do if you'd like a career in management consulting? First, get a good education. Business school is a good place to start; information technology is another good route. Keep in mind that the best consulting jobs go to the brightest students, so pay attention to your grades.

Another thing to consider is how to sell yourself—your knowledge, your personality, and your skills. So what are the ingredients most likely to lead to success? It helps to be outgoing, to like people, and to work well in teams. It certainly doesn't hurt to be a good decision-maker, to be flexible, and to be easygoing. It's important to respond to situations with logic, objectivity, and empathy. Good instincts are a must.

The consulting business has grown at an amazing rate in recent years. Global competition, technological advances, and constantly changing business practices have resulted in many opportunities for management consultants. There's no sign of a slowdown either.

TRY IT OUT

TELL THE STORY

Storyboarding is a technique perfected by Walt Disney (see Get Acquainted interview that follows). It involved getting everyone on a project team to display their plans on the walls. That way everyone knows what everyone else is doing, and it helps everyone visualize what the project is all about.

You can try a modified version of storyboarding. All you need is a pad of those little sticky notes or some squares of scrap paper and tape. Pick one of the following ideas and see if you can use the paper to visualize all the steps.

- ☼ a new way to organize the cafeteria so you don't have to stand in line so long
- ☼ ideas for adding more free time to the school day without giving up any learning time
- ☼ a plan to keep your room tidy enough to keep your parents happy

💡 a plan for a kid-friendly school, including the types of classes you would offer, the daily schedule, and requirements for teachers

💡 suggestions for things your family can do to enjoy time together

Write one idea or suggestion on each square of paper. Arrange (and rearrange) them on a wall to figure out the best solutions. Under each idea, add squares of paper that list each step required to make the solution work.

GET THE INSIDE SCOOP

If you're really interested in finding out more about the field of management consulting, you may want to take a look at some of the following resources. They can help point you in the right direction.

Alpert, Gary, and Steve Pollack. *So You Want to Be a Management Consultant.* San Francisco: WetFeet Press, 2000.

Butler, Timothy, and James Waldroop. *Discovering Your Career In Business.* New York: Perseus Press, 1997.

Dehi, Jason. *Careers in Management Consulting.* Boston: Harvard Business School Publishing, 1999.

Management Consulting: Exploring the Field, Finding the Right Job, and Landing It. Boston: Harvard Business School Publishing, 1997.

Naficy, Mariam. *The Fast Track: The Insider's Guide to Careers in Management Consulting, Investment Banking and Securities Trading.* New York: Broadway Books, 1997.

Stair, Lila B. *Careers in Business.* Lincolnwood, Ill.: VGM Publishing, 1998.

THE BEST OF THE BEST

Following are the website addresses of some of the top management consulting firms in the world. Take a look at their sites and see if you can figure out the specialties of each firm:

◊ Andersen Consulting at http://www.ac.com
◊ Cap Gemini Group at http://www.capgemini.com
◊ CSC at http://www.css.com
◊ Deloitte Consulting at http://www.dc.com
◊ Ernst and Young at http://www.eyi.com
◊ KPMG at http://www.kpmg.com
◊ McKinsey & Company at http://www.mckinsey.com
◊ Mercer Consulting Group at http://www.mercer.com
◊ Price Waterhouse Coopers at http://www.pwcglobal.com

CYBER CONSULTING

There are some very informative websites that can help give you a better idea of what management consulting is all about. Among the best websites are:

◊ Management Consulting Online at http://www.cob. ohio-state/edu/~opler/cons/mco.html.
◊ Wet Feet's Consulting Industry Quick at http://www. wetfeet.com/industries/quicks/consulting-online2.asp.

GOOD ADVICE FOR HIRE

A good way to get some experience consulting is with the peer mediation programs that are springing up in schools all over the country. The programs train students to help other students resolve problems. Find out if your school has one and get involved.

Another way to get some experience is to volunteer to tutor younger students. If you are especially good in a certain subject, you can share your knowledge with other students. Even reading stories and helping younger kids with their homework can give you some "consulting" experience.

CHECK IT OUT

American Management
   Association
1601 Broadway
New York, New York 10019
http://www.amanet.org

Association of Management
   Consulting Firms
521 Fifth Avenue,
   35th Floor
New York, New York 10175-3598

Institute of Management
  Consultants
521 5th Avenue, 35th Floor
New York, New York 10175-3598
http://www.imcusa.org

National Association of
  Management Consultants
4200 Wisconsin NW,
  Suite 106
Washington, D.C. 20016

GET ACQUAINTED

Bill Capodagli and
Lynn Jackson,
Management Consultants

CAREER PATH

CHILDHOOD ASPIRATIONS:
For Bill it was to become an
orchestra leader. Lynn wanted to
be an actor and scriptwriter.

FIRST JOBS: Bill got his start
delivering handbills and catalogs
for a penny each when he was
about 10 years old. Lynn did a
lot of baby-sitting when she
was younger.

CURRENT JOBS: Cofounders and partners in
Capodagli Jackson Consulting.

PARTNERS IN SUCCESS

Bill Capodagli learned what business was all about at an early
age. His parents owned a little shop that sold toys, tobacco
products, and newspapers. The store was open 365 days a
year, which gave Capodagli plenty of firsthand experience in
what it takes to run a business. The experience made him
curious about how other businesses worked.

After graduating from college, Capodagli started his career
in business by crunching numbers for an insurance firm. Soon
realizing that he preferred working with people to working

with a calculator, he gladly accepted an offer to join the company's internal consulting group. And that's how he got his start in management consulting more than 25 years ago.

Things were a little different for Lynn Jackson. She took her longtime interests in acting and writing and put them to work in business. She started out working in the human resources department of a company. There she was responsible for training employees and writing business manuals. She found that all her "theatrics" came in handy when trying to keep an audience interested in business topics.

When their business paths crossed, Capodagli and Jackson realized that their talents combined to create an interesting mix of skills and expertise. They started a consulting firm and worked with many big corporations before deciding that writing a book would give them more credibility.

WHAT'S MICKEY MOUSE GOT TO DO WITH IT?

Since their work gave them the inside track in some of the biggest and most famous companies in America, Capodagli and Jackson started looking at the ingredients that made for success in business. One company in particular kept showing up on all their "best companies" lists. Production, creativity, training, customer service, employee turnover—this company was a top performer in all the things that mattered most. The company? None other than Disney!

Founder Walt Disney built a multibillion-dollar empire on the foundation of a cartoon mouse. He did it by believing in his dreams and daring to make them come true.

Capodagli and Jackson had a hunch that the same business principles that worked for Disney could work for other types of businesses as well. So they started compiling lots of data and got permission to get a firsthand, behind-the-scenes look at how the Disney business was run on a day-to-day basis.

They were able to test their "hunch" by introducing the Disney principles of success to a variety of major corporations. And the ideas worked! They were effective in publishing houses, companies that made and sold refrigerators and stoves, oil and gas companies, utility companies—companies that had nothing at all in common except applying the Disney principles to their way of doing business.

The book came next. It's called *The Disney Way* (McGraw-Hill, 1999). It outlines 10 business principles that have brought the Disney company phenomenal success, such as empowerment and attention to detail. The book's success has completely transformed Capodagli and Jackson's firm. They used to spend 90 percent of their time working with businesses and 10 percent of their time giving speeches and conducting seminars. They now spend 90 percent of their time writing and speaking and only 10 percent of their time consulting. But that means they get the chance to reach even more businesses. And the fat checks that come from giving all those speeches aren't so bad either.

KID-SIZED SUCCESS
Capodagli and Jackson have another hunch. They think that kids can learn as much from Disney as businesses can. Here are their secrets of success for kids:

Dream—What do you really enjoy doing? What do you like doing so much that it doesn't seem like work? That's where you find the best ingredients for dreams.

Believe—Write down the values that are most important to you. How do you want to live your life? What do you hope to accomplish?

Dare—Do what it takes to make your dreams come true. It might not be easy. It may even mean that you'll have to start now by studying hard and getting good grades!

Do—Make a plan and go for it!

P.S.
You can find out more about Capodagli and Jackson's business and the issues they work with at their website. Go to http://www.capojac.com.

Publisher

SHORTCUTS

GO to a bookstore and look at all the different kinds of books. Look for a specific genre (if you don't know what that word means, look it up) such as mysteries, children's books, inspirational books, and business books.

READ *Publishers Weekly*, the number-one place for information on the publishing industry. Find the on-line version at http://www.pubweekly.com or look for the latest issue at a bookstore.

TRY seeing if your favorite childhood books made the New York Public Library's list of "100 Picture Books Everyone Should Know" at http://www.nypl.org/branch/kids/gloria.html.

SKILL SET

✔ WRITING

✔ TALKING

✔ MONEY

WHAT IS A PUBLISHER?

It all started with the invention of moveable type by Johannes Gutenberg and his publication of the Bible in the mid-1400s. Since then, the publishing industry has blossomed to include all kinds of mediums—books, magazines, newspapers, CD-ROMs, and even electronic publishing. And behind all these words are publishers, who make it all happen.

In a traditional sense, a publisher is the biggest boss in a publishing company. He or she is ultimately responsible for deciding the overall direction the company will take. That means they decide if the company will specialize in children's books or sports books, a magazine for new parents, or whatever. Once the company's niche is established, the publisher generally has the final say in what books or other products are produced for each publishing season (publishers typically release new products in fall and spring catalogs). Maybe the most important responsibility that many publishers assume is putting up the money that it takes to acquire, print, market, and distribute the products published by their company. The

old adage that you have to spend money in order to make money is certainly true for publishers.

With between 46,000 and 53,000 new books published each year, more than 18,500 magazines published on a regular basis, and a wide variety of daily and weekly newspapers in operation, there is plenty of opportunity for people looking to make a living with words. However you won't be walking out of high school or college and land the top spot in a publishing house. Not a chance. You are much more likely to work your way up through the ranks in the editorial, marketing, sales, or production departments of a publishing company. Working toward that top job is a goal worth pursuing and something to be proud of once you make it.

There are some interesting things happening in this industry that may have an impact on your future career in publishing. First is the way that a handful of publishers have swallowed up a big chunk of the smaller houses to become megapub-

lishers. They are so big, in fact, that it is estimated that just six of these big publishers capture about 60 percent of revenues earned on adult books. Second is a growing trend among entrepreneurial authors and publishers to buck the traditional publishing system and "do it their way." They are generally known as "self-publishers."

According to self-publishing experts Tom and Marilyn Ross, self-publishers "are sometimes called private publishers, independent publishers, small presses, or alternative publishers. But whatever label they may wear, they are in a word 'mavericks,' and they are part of a larger whole known as the small press movement—which, by the way, is growing at a breathtaking rate and has achieved not only respectability but extraordinary results."

Self-publishers are often authors who decide to publish their own work. Sometimes they tap into a specific niche such as crafts or health and publish a variety of related titles. The Internet is, of course, bringing new opportunities for innovative self-publishers too. Although it's almost impossible to keep track of how many self-publishers are at work, some say that there may well be as many as 55,000. Some are wildly successful and sell lots of books. Others are making a decent living, and others are losing money.

Like traditional publishers, the self-publishers who are making a big splash have two things in common. First, they publish books that other people want to read. It seems pretty obvious, but one of most common mistakes publishers make is writing or publishing books that *they* want to write or read. Successful publishers of all sizes must first and foremost answer this question: Who wants to read this book?

Besides publishing quality books, all successful publishers also know how to sell their books. It's been said that bookstores are one of the worst places to sell a book. You can't expect to put a book in a store with thousands of other books and expect yours to fly off the shelf. Instead, publishers have to create a demand for their books. They do this through marketing, publicity, and specially crafted sales strategies. It's the only way to win the publishing game.

So what should you do if you want a future in books? Suggestion number one: Read everything you can get your hands on—books, magazines, newspapers, even websites. Just read! Suggestion number two: Consider pursuing a degree in English, literature, journalism, or marketing to get your foot in the door of the profession. Suggestion number three: Get some experience with an established publisher. Try working in different departments to get a good look at all aspects of the publishing process. If your ultimate ambition is to someday start your own publishing company or to run an established house, do what you can to build your business skills. Some of the activities that follow will help you get started.

TRY IT OUT

THE BEST OF THE BEST

Books are big business. In 1999, a whopping $13.7 billion was spent in the United States on books. A nice chunk of this income came from sales of books found on best-seller lists. *The New York Times* publishes one of the most famous best-seller lists every Sunday, and publishers everywhere want to land a book on that list. Find out what books are making it big by picking up a copy of the Sunday edition of the *New York Times* at a local bookstore or newsstand. Another way to find the list is to check the Sunday book section of your local paper. You may also want to see what major booksellers such as Barnes and Noble and Amazon.com have to say about the biggies. You can find their lists at http://www.bn.com or http://www.amazon.com.

While you're at it, make up your own version of a "best-seller" list. Number a sheet of paper from 1 to 10, and list your all-time favorite books with the best one at the top of the list. Do any of the books on your list match the ones on the best-seller lists you found in the paper or on the Internet?

ON-LINE BOOK STUFF

The following websites are for real publishing professionals, so they aren't exactly filled with fun and games for kids.

However, they can give you an idea of the types of resources that publishers use to do their jobs. Here are some of the best:

Book Wire   http://www.bookwire.com includes book industry news, reviews, author interviews, thousands of links to other book-related sites, and more.

PubNet 2000   http://www.pubnet.org provides links to thousands of book publishers, suppliers, and distributors.

Another great site is one hosted by the American Library Association (ALA), which keeps track of notable children's websites, many of which are connected to books or authors. Find the latest list at http://www.ala.org/alsc/ ncwc.html.

GET PUBLISHED!

If your plan is to someday publish other people's writing, you might want to get yourself published first. Right now. There are plenty of opportunities for kids just like you to see their writing in print. The Internet is one place to share your best work. Here are some websites where you can submit your writing and read the writing of other kids from all over the world:

- ☼ Kidsworld @ http://www.beconnex.net/kidsworld features jokes, games, and stories written by kids and for kids.
- ☼ Kid's Story @ http://www.kidstory.com is a fun place to share your stories and poems or just hang out to play some games.
- ☼ MidLink Magazine @ http://www.longwood.cs.ucf.edu/ ~MidLink offers cyberspace for students to share their very best writing.
- ☼ KidLit @ http://www.mgfx.com/kidlit/index.htm is another website that features literature and art produced by kids of various ages.
- ☼ KidPub @ http://www.kidpub.org is an award-winning website featuring more than 36,000 stories written by kids from all over the planet.

There are also a number of publications that publish writing by young authors. Write or check the websites of the following publications to ask about their guidelines.

Children's Express
1440 New York Avenue NW,
    Suite 510
Washington, D.C. 20005
http://www.cenews.org

Cobblestone
20 Grove Street
Peterborough, New Hampshire
    03458
http://www.cobblestonepub.com

Jack and Jill
P.O. Box 567
Indianapolis, Indiana 46206

Stone Soup
Box 83
Santa Cruz, California 95063
http://www.stonesoup.com

WHO WROTE IT?

Write a Mystery! is a really fun site for mystery lovers. Investigate this very popular publishing genre and write your own mystery in the process. The website is http://www.the-case.com.

IN GOOD COMPANY

What do Huckleberry Finn, Tarzan, and the C-A-N-D-Y Monster all have in common? They were originally characters in self-published books by their respective authors: Mark Twain, Edgar Rice Burroughs, and Vicki Lansky.

Now it's your turn. If you really want to find out what it's like to publish a book, just do it. Think of a really good idea that people in your "world" might buy. Maybe it's a directory of after-school activities or summer fun programs. How about a cookbook full of favorite recipes from kids and teachers at your school? Think of a good idea and make sure to ask yourself that all-important question: Who would want to read a book like this? Possible customers might be other kids in your class, the school PTA, relatives, neighbors, libraries in your community, and so on.

CHECK IT OUT

American Society of Magazine
  Editors
919 Third Avenue, 22nd Floor
New York, New York 10022
http://asme.magazine.org

Association of American
  Publishers
71 Fifth Avenue
New York, New York 10003
http://www.publishers.org

Audio Publishers Association
627 Aviation Way
Manhattan Beach, California
  90266
http://www.audiopub.org

Magazine Publishers of America
919 Third Avenue
New York, New York 10022
http://www.magazine.org

National Newspaper
  Association
1010 Glebe Road, Suite 450
Arlington, Virginia 22201
http://www.nna.org

Publishers Marketing
  Association
627 Aviation Way
Manhattan Beach, California
  90266
http://www.pma-online.org

GET ACQUAINTED

Cheryl Barnes, Publisher

CAREER PATH

CHILDHOOD ASPIRATION: To do something artistic.

FIRST JOB: Working in an architectural firm.

CURRENT JOB: Copublisher of VSP Books, a company specializing in illustrated books for children about special and historic places.

THE DYNAMIC DUO

As copublisher along with her husband Peter, Cheryl Shaw Barnes wears a lot of hats. She helps write the books, she

often illustrates them, she visits schools to talk about her books, she goes to bookstores to sign her books, she does everything she can think of to sell more books, and until recently she even packed the books up to send to customers. That's the way it goes for an independent publisher, but, according to the Barneses, it is worth it.

Their company, VSP Books, has published 13 books and a couple of teacher's guides. By publishing the books themselves, the Barneses estimate that they earn 300 to 400 percent more than they would if they let someone else publish their books for them.

They like the extra income as well as the control they have over their books. Doing everything themselves allows them to give each title the same tender loving care they would give to a new baby—well, almost. At the very least, they can be sure that the books are produced with the quality their reputation rests on, and that the books get the best of all chances to find their way into the hands of young readers.

THE WEIRDEST THING HAPPENED

VSP Books came about in an unusual way. Barnes and her husband were vacationing one summer on Nantucket Island in Massachusetts when they overheard someone ask a gift shop owner for a children's book about the island. The owner told them there wasn't one. The idea for a publishing company was born, and their first book launched soon afterward. The book, *Nat, Nat, the Nantucket Cat,* continues to sell several thousand copies each year in just a handful of shops frequented by tourists.

It's a formula that has worked for other "destination" books as well, including *Alexander the Old Town Mouse* about historic Alexandria, Virginia; *Martha's Vineyard* about the scenic island in Massachusetts; and *Cornelius Vandermouse, the Pride of Newport,* about historic Newport, Rhode Island.

If the publishing company itself came about in an unusual way, the Barneses' turn toward publishing books about the government came about in a really strange way. One afternoon, Barnes was enjoying watching one of her daughters

play lacrosse when a woman, the mother of another player, came stomping across the field toward her. The woman, who had worked in the administrations of Presidents George Bush and Ronald Reagan, told Barnes, "I know what book you're going to do next." Barnes thought that was rather odd since *she* didn't even know what book she was going to do next, but the woman seemed fairly certain. It turns out that part of the woman's job involved choosing gifts for foreign dignitaries and their families. She had decided that she was tired of giving fake handcuffs from the FBI to the children of these visitors, and she wanted a book about the White House to give instead. Impressed with the quality of Barnes's previous books, the woman thought that Barnes was the right choice to create a delightful book about the "people's" house.

Before Barnes knew it, she was off to the White House with a fancy camera to take pictures of every nook and cranny. She used the pictures to illustrate *Woodrow, the White House Mouse,* the book she and her husband wove around the presidency and America's most famous house.

One thing led to another after that. Someone from the Capitol called and wanted a book about Congress. The result was *House Mouse, Senate Mouse.* They couldn't leave out the third branch of the federal government, so *Marshall, the Courthouse Mouse* was soon to follow. One of their latest books, *Woodrow for President,* explains the electoral process in an easy-to-understand and hard-to-forget way.

YOU KNOW YOU'VE MADE IT WHEN . . .

An episode of *The Rosie O'Donnell Show* proved that Barnes was doing a good job getting the word out about their books. One day Barnes was sitting in her home office signing books, packing orders, and halfway paying attention to Rosie's show when one of her assistants pointed to the television. There on the show a very important guest was giving a copy of *Woodrow, the White House Mouse* as a gift to Rosie's son. The guest was none other than First Lady Hillary Clinton. It was a nice surprise and a wonderful bit of free publicity for Barnes's books.

THE LITTLE ENGINE THAT COULD

When Barnes was a child, her favorite book was *The Little Engine That Could.* She could relate to that plucky little engine that worked so hard to get up the hill. That's because Barnes is dyslexic, and she had a really hard time learning to read. In fact, she didn't learn how to read until she was in the third grade. It was a hard thing to deal with because all the other kids could already read. Fortunately, she had some good teachers who helped her build up her confidence while her brain was working hard to catch up with the other kids. One teacher in particular helped her discover her very special abilities as an artist.

Barnes says her learning disability turned out to be a good thing in her life. It made her work harder and gave her a strength she wouldn't have otherwise had—traits that come in handy as she continues to create wonderful books and build a publishing business.

P.S.

You can find out more about Barnes and her books at http://www.vspbooks.com. Or cast your vote for the winning big cheese at http://www.woodrowforpresident.com.

Real Estate Agent

SHORTCUTS

SKILL SET

✔ MONEY

✔ TALKING

✔ MATH

GO visit "open house" models in a new sub-division or apartment building.

READ the free real estate magazines often found in racks at grocery stores or news stands to find out the going rate for your dream house.

TRY figuring out how much the monthly payments would be for a $1,000,000 house. Use the calculator at http://www.nt. mortgage101.com for help.

WHAT IS A REAL ESTATE AGENT?

A real estate agent knows property—where it is, how much it's worth, and how to buy or sell it. An agent may specialize in residential property (places where people live), commercial property (places where people work), or resort property (places where people play). Some agents do business in a particular community or city, while others cover a broader geographic region or specific type of property. Still others work internationally and handle property transactions in a certain part of the world such as a European country or in resort areas such as the Caribbean.

Whether they deal with condominiums or skyscrapers, most realtors work both sides of the "game"—they either work with people who want to buy property or those who want to sell it. Either way, the challenge is to find the right match—the perfect place for someone to buy or the perfect person to buy a place. To do this successfully, real estate agents must know a lot about both property and people. They must be knowledgeable about things such as zoning laws, mortgage rates, financing options, tax rates, and insurance coverage. They must be able to listen to what their clients say about what they are looking for (which sometimes means reading between the lines) and find homes or business properties that meet their needs and budgets.

Even the most basic real estate transactions tend to be fairly complicated. Just selling or buying a house can involve piles of paperwork. There are contracts, deeds, disclosures, financial statements, and all kinds of other legal documents. Computers play an important part in helping real estate professionals manage the paperwork, and they help agents keep track of market trends and available properties.

Agents also use computers to conduct region-wide or even worldwide searches for property that matches a client's criteria. Clients tell an agent exactly what they want; the agent clicks a few buttons and out comes a list of properties that match the clients' needs. Talk about the ultimate in matchmaking! Things have gotten so fancy that you can even take a "virtual tour" of a property on-line. You can sit in front of a computer screen and see inside a house thousands of miles away.

While being an agent is probably the first career that comes to mind when you think of real estate, there are actually many interesting professions related to the sale, management, and analysis of property.

Appraisers investigate the quality of a given piece of property to determine its value. They do this by gathering information about the property, taking measurements, interviewing people familiar with the property's history, and searching public records of sales, leases, and other transactions. They also compare the property with other similar properties to come up with a fair estimate of the property's value. Appraisers compile their findings into a report for a bank or other type of financial lending institution. A bank will not loan money on a property unless its appraised value meets or exceeds the loan amount, so this process is important to buyers and sellers alike.

Loan officers are the "money" people who typically work for banks or mortgage companies and help arrange financing for people or businesses who are purchasing property.

Property managers take care of other people's or companies' real estate investments. They might manage any number of residential homes, apartments or condominiums, office buildings, retail stores, or industrial properties. Their duties typically include handling the financial dealings of the property—paying bills and taxes and collecting rents. They may also handle all the day-to-day matters involved in keeping a property clean and well cared for. Property managers or management companies are paid by the owners of the property.

Property developers are entrepreneurs who buy land and turn it into neighborhoods, resorts, or office complexes. A good property developer can look at an empty field and see a bustling community. It takes vision, an ability to manage big projects, a knowledge of building and construction techniques, and money—lots of it.

While some people go into real estate or appraising with little more than a high school diploma, others have college degrees in areas such as business, management, or real estate management. But no one goes into real estate or appraising without the proper certification. Certification usually involves passing a test and other requirements by a professional organization such as the National Association of Realtors.

Success in any career in real estate tends to hinge on a couple of common traits. One trait is an entrepreneurial spirit. Many real estate careers offer unique opportunities to do your own thing and be your own boss. In fact, it is the flexible nature of the work that draws many people to the profession. Essentially, real estate agents work as hard as they want to work, choose how many (or how few) hours they want to devote to their work, and reap the results accordingly. Obviously, the harder (and the smarter) they work, the more income they earn.

Experience is another common trait. It takes time to build up a client base and to learn the ropes in real estate. You can expect to find lots of experience—and a little luck—behind the most successful people in this business.

Maybe the most important trait of a real estate agent is the ability to "close the deal." This involves negotiating with clients to work out arrangements that suit everyone. It takes people skills and communication skills, and you won't make it far in this profession without them.

TRY IT OUT

VIRTUAL TOURS

The Internet has opened new doors in real estate. For instance, if you live in Dallas and have just learned that your new job promotion means you'll have to relocate to Los Angeles, you can sit in front of your computer and find a new home on the Internet. At least that's how it works in theory. Most people still want to have an old-fashioned look at the actual property. But virtual tours of the property can save everyone a lot of time and effort. It's also a great way for you to learn more about the real estate business.

Use the following websites to compare the costs of a four- or five-bedroom luxury home in at least three different parts of the country.

☼ http://www.realestate.com
☼ http://www.hometours.com
☼ http://www.bamboo.com/index.shtml

Print out pictures of the properties you find and make a chart showcasing where you can get the most house for the least money.

A REAL ESTATE READING LIST

For more information about careers in real estate, try some of the following resources:

_____

Edwards, Kenneth W. *Your Successful Real Estate Career.* New York: Amacom, 1997.

Evans, Mariwyn. *Opportunities in Property Management.* Lincolnwood, Ill.: VGM Career Horizons, 2000.

———. *Opportunities in Real Estate.* Lincolnwood, Ill.: VGM Career Horizons, 1993.

Janik, Carolyn. *Making Money in Real Estate.* New York: Kiplinger Books, 2000.

Janik, Carolyn, and Ruth Regnis. *Real Estate Careers: 25 Growing Opportunities.* New York: John Wiley, 1994.

Masi, Mary. *Real Estate Career Starter: Launch a Lucrative and Fulfilling Career.* New York: Learning Express, 1998.

For the inside scoop on what potential clients need to look for in a new home, read:

Fields, Alan, and Denise Fields. *Your New House.* Boulder, Colo.: Windsor Peak Press, 1994.

_____

REAL ESTATE HOMEWORK

The local school system is one thing that many families consider when looking for a new home. What if you were trying to sell a home in your neighborhood? What could you tell your client about the nearby schools?

Make a list of the preschools, elementary schools, middle schools, and high schools that kids in your neighborhood attend. Find out any special features about each school to make a good "sales pitch." For instance, the elementary school has a brand-new computer center, the high school has a winning football team, the middle school has the highest test scores in the area—all the things people tend to brag about.

For some official information, see what you can find about these schools at The School Report (http://theschoolreport.com), a website offering nationwide statistics on schools and frequently used by real estate professionals. Gathering this type of information is called market research and would be an important part of a career in real estate.

REAL ESTATE MATCHMAKING

Matching people with properties is, in a nutshell, what the real estate business is all about. Give your matchmaking skills a workout with the following activity. First, gather a couple of real estate magazines, the real estate classified advertising section from Sunday's newspaper, and any resources you can find that include pictures of houses and other types of buildings.

Now, read these client profiles carefully.

- ☼ Family of four, both parents work in the city, one child is in elementary school, the other child is a toddler. Need three or four bedrooms, at least two bathrooms, and an attached garage. Looking for a family-friendly neighborhood with good schools and child-care options.
- ☼ Retired couple, wife is in a wheelchair, looking for nice, affordable, one-story home in a quiet area. New construction is desirable in order to easily accommodate wife's disability.
- ☼ New software business looking for 5,000 square feet of office space in downtown area or business park with easy access to major roads. A "build to suit" situation would be ideal.
- ☼ Single person in mid-20s, just landed a great new job, looking for a "cool" place to call home. Must have lots of amenities for active social life including clubhouse, pool, and workout facilities.

Designate a separate sheet of paper for each situation and attach pictures of homes and properties as well as classified advertisements that might interest each client.

CHECK IT OUT

American Industrial Real Estate Association
700 South Flower Street, Suite 600
Los Angeles, California 90017
http://www.airea.com

American Real Estate and Urban Economics Association
Indiana University, Kelley School of Business
1309 East Tenth Street, Suite 738
Bloomington, Indiana 47405
http://www.areuea.org

Center for Real Estate and Urban Economic Studies
University of Connecticut
School of Business Administration
368 Fairfield Road, U-41RE
Storrs, Connecticut 06269-2041
http://www.sba.uconn.edu

National Association of Corporate Real Estate Executives
440 Columbia Drive, Suite 100
West Palm Beach, Florida 33409
http://www.nacore.org

National Association of Industrial and Office Properties
2201 Cooperative Way, Third Floor
Hendron, Virginia 20171
http://www.naiop.org

National Association of Real Estate Brokers
1629 K Street NW, Suite 602
Washington, D.C. 20006
http://www.nareb.com

National Association of Realtors
430 North Michigan Avenue
Chicago, Illinois 60611
http://www.realtor.com

Society of Industrial and Office Realtors
700 11th Street NW, Suite 510
Washington, D.C. 20001
http://www.sior.com

GET ACQUAINTED

Nishat Karimi,
Real Estate Agent

CAREER PATH

CHILDHOOD ASPIRATION:
Wanted to be a doctor until all the blood grossed her out.

FIRST JOB: Sales clerk at a boutique in a mall.

CURRENT JOB: Real estate agent specializing in residential sales with the Henry S. Miller Company.

MIXING CAREERS AND REAL LIFE

Nishat Karimi graduated from college with a degree in business administration. She started her career working in marketing for the May Company and worked her way up to area sales manager before she and her husband decided to start a family. Although she really enjoyed the work, the job involved quite a bit of travel and long hours. So once the babies started coming, Karimi quit her job to take care of them.

As the children got older Karimi decided it was time to go back to work. However, she didn't want a job that would lock her into a full-time schedule. She wanted a job with flexible hours that she could do from home.

That's when Karimi found out about real estate. It looked like a good fit with her business and marketing background, and it would allow her to keep her home and work responsibilities more balanced. To get started, Karimi had to take special courses in real estate—one on the basics, another on contracts, and another in finance. Then she had to pass an exam in order to qualify for a real estate license.

Even with a license, new agents have to work under a certified real estate broker, so Karimi signed up with a big, independent real estate company working in the Dallas/Forth Worth area. Even though she works for a big company, Karimi is in business for herself. No one tells her when and how long she has to work, and no one tells her what to do or how to run her business. Karimi decides all that for herself. But the company does provide things such as office space, a solid reputation, and other perks. They don't provide these things for free, of course, but the arrangement works out well for both Karimi and the real estate company.

FINDING A NICHE
Originally from Pakistan, Karimi speaks the Hindi language fluently. Karimi uses this skill to market her services to the many South Asian people relocating to Dallas. Because she knows the language and understands the customs of these home buyers, many of whom are in the United States for the first time, she is able to help them in ways other agents cannot. Her background provides a natural "in" with a growing segment of the metropolitan Dallas population and adds a very profitable international angle to her business. Karimi believes this edge is one reason why she recently was named "rookie of the year" at her company.

THE REAL STORY ABOUT REAL ESTATE
Karimi is quick to dispel the myth that all real estate agents are rich. Sure, making a lot of money is possible—and highly desirable. But it takes a lot of hard work and time to build up a good base of clients. Real estate agents have to get the word out that they are in business.

Having worked in the business for a couple years now, Karimi is still building that base and spends a good chunk of her time prospecting for clients—through special mailings, hosting open houses, advertising on Hindi-language radio stations, and letting everyone she meets know that she is a Realtor. She says that satisfied clients are really her best forms of advertising. If she does a good job for someone, they will tell their friends and their friends will come to her when they need to buy or sell a house.

FEAST OR FAMINE

Real estate agents do not get a paycheck every week. Instead, they get a commission from each property that they sell (usually about 3 percent per agent for buyer and seller). This is good news and bad news. The good news is that when agents do sell a property, they can earn some pretty big bucks (upwards of $5,000–$10,000 per sale). The bad news is: no sales, no pay. Karimi says that during certain parts of the year, such as spring and summer, things are so hectic that it's all she can do to keep up with the business. Other times, such as the winter months, she feels as though she spends a lot of time twiddling her thumbs. This part of her job makes Karimi especially glad that she has a background in business. She is careful to invest her earnings so that they stretch to cover the slow times.

Her business background also comes in handy when it comes to planning her business strategies. So far, Karimi's goal has been to double her sales every year, and so far she has done just that. At this pace, Karimi is well on her way to becoming a real estate superstar!

FYI

You can find out more about Karimi's work at her website at http://www.northdallasproperties.com.

Sales Representative

SHORTCUTS

SKILL SET

✔ TALKING

✔ MONEY

✔ TRAVEL

GO watch sales representatives in action at a car dealership, an upscale fashion store, and a fast-food restaurant. Can you see a difference in their style and methods?

READ Zig Ziglar's *Secrets of Closing the Sale* (New York: HarperCollins, 1992).

TRY volunteering to help sell ads for your school yearbook or candy for a sports booster club.

WHAT IS A SALES REPRESENTATIVE?

If someone can make it, someone else can sell it. This fact makes for an awful lot of variety in the sales profession. Sales representatives (or "reps") sell every product imaginable from candy to computer hardware, from eyeglass frames to sophisticated medical equipment.

One of the most obvious places to find a sales representative is in a retail shop at the local mall. There is plenty of opportunity in retail sales, although it is not exceptionally profitable for sales clerks working behind the counter.

The picture changes for sales reps who work for the companies that provide products for retail stores to sell. Called wholesaling or trade sales, this type of work generally involves covering a specific geographic territory, making sales and serving clients. Since these positions can involve selling an entire product line and larger volumes of products, the earning potential is greater.

Traveling sales representatives also work for almost any imaginable type of business, selling both products and services. They are an extremely important part of a company's "image," because the sales rep is often the only person from a particular firm that a client ever meets.

Industrial sales involves selling parts or materials used to manufacture other products. This type of selling can get pretty complicated, so sales reps tend to have a technical background in the particular industry they are selling to.

One more type of sales is called new business selling. This type of selling includes positions in real estate companies, bank loan departments, brokerage firms, and insurance companies. This is another type of sales that can require specialized training.

The sales profession sometimes gets a bad rap. People associate the old door-to-door sales mentality or the image of a used car salesperson with the profession. These stereotypes revolve around a fast-talking huckster, someone who would pretty much do or say anything to make a sale, regardless of whether it was true or not. However, this is not how truly

professional (and very successful) sales representatives play the game. Instead they provide good service and quality products to their clients. They learn to match genuine needs and wants with appropriate products and services through careful research. For them, manipulation is not a rule of thumb. They sell products they can be proud of and conduct themselves in a friendly and businesslike manner.

In many cases, sales reps work on commission, which means that instead of receiving a regular paycheck, they receive a percentage of income from every item they sell. Commissions can mean good news and bad news for sales reps. If sales are good, the pay is good. If sales are down, so is the pay. Some people find the idea of working on commission to be a real motivation. Other people find it stressful. Perhaps the best scenario is one that offers a generous base pay with bonuses for reaching specific sales goals. The method of pay is definitely something to consider if you decide to go into sales.

Training requirements run the gamut from high school diplomas and on-the-job training to college degrees in areas such as liberal arts, social science, business, or management. The educational route you take depends a lot on the type of products you sell and the type of company you hope to work for.

Professions related to sales include marketing, advertising, and public relations. All offer a different twist on selling ideas, services, products, or companies, and they each provide a variety of ways to grow a career. Sales can also be one method of getting your foot in the door of a particular industry so you can work your way into other types of positions.

When you think about it, nobody would be in business for long without someone to help sell their products. So a good sales force is vital to a business. If you enjoy meeting people, are a good listener, aren't easily intimidated by rejection (there will always be people who won't want what you have to sell, no matter how good a salesperson you may be), and aren't afraid to work hard, consider starting your career in sales.

TRY IT OUT

SECRETS OF SUCCESS

Zig Ziglar—a super salesman, famous motivational speaker, and author—says that great salespeople are made, not born. He believes that there are five keys to successful selling:

- ☼ Prospecting, or identifying who can and will buy what you have to sell
- ☼ Presenting or knowing the product and showing it in a way that makes people want to buy it
- ☼ Closing, or getting people to say "yes, I want to buy your product"
- ☼ Following up, or staying in touch with customers
- ☼ Positive self-image, or having what it takes to succeed in sales

Imagine how you could use these steps to sell a product that you like to use, maybe a favorite cereal or soft drink. How about a favorite game or sports gear? Ask yourself who would want to buy that sort of product. What can you say about the product to make them want to buy it? What can you do to make it easy for them to say yes? How would you stay in touch with these potential customers? And, last of all, how can present yourself in a confident way?

You can read more about Ziglar's ideas in his book *5 Steps to Successful Selling* (New York: Simon & Schuster, 1995).

SELL YOURSELF ON A CAREER IN SALES

There are lots of ways to make a living in sales. Books like these will give you a better idea of where the jobs are.

Basye, Anne. *Opportunities in Telemarketing Careers.* Lincolnwood, Ill.: VGM Career Horizons, 1994.

Camenson, Blythe, and Jan Goldberg. *Real People Working in Sales and Marketing.* Lincolnwood, Ill.: VGM Career Horizons, 1996.

Ellis, Chad Wayne. *Opportunities in Medical Sales Careers.* Lincolnwood, Ill.: VGM Career Horizons, 1997.

Lipow, Valerie. *Retailing Career Starter: Move Ahead in This Fast Growing Field.* New York: Learning Express, 1998.

SELLING WITH A FULL DECK

If you would like a good trial run of what it's like to be in sales, find out if your school (or high school) offers a program through the Distributive Education Clubs of America (DECA). It's an education program that helps prepare students for entrepreneurial, marketing, or management careers. For more information write to DECA at 1908 Association Drive, Reston, Virginia 22090, or visit their website at http://www.deca.org.

CHECK IT OUT

American Marketing Association
250 South Wacker Drive
Chicago, Illinois 60606
http://www.ama.org

Direct Marketing Association
11 West 42nd Street
New York, New York 10036-8096
http://www.the-dma.org

Direct Selling Association
1776 K Street NW
Washington, D.C. 20006
http://www.dsa.org

National Association of General Merchandise Representatives
401 North Michigan Avenue
Chicago, Illinois 60611-4267
http://www.nagmr.org

National Retail Federation
325 7th Street NW, Suite 1100
Washington, D.C. 20004
http://www.nrf.com

Sales and Marketing Executives International
Career Education Division
5500 Interstate North Parkway, Suite 545
Atlanta, Georgia 30328
http://www.smei.org

GET ACQUAINTED

Ronn Cordova,
Sales Representative

CAREER PATH

CHILDHOOD ASPIRATION: To be an architect.

FIRST JOB: Cashier at a gas station.

CURRENT JOB: Director of franchise development, Little Gym International.

YOU OUGHT TO BE IN SALES

Ronn Cordova didn't go looking for a job in sales. It came looking for him. Inspired by Mr. Brady on *The Brady Bunch* television show, Cordova had planned to be an architect. He graduated from high school, got four years of special training in college, and spent 11 years working as a draftsman. His job was to draw blueprints for a heating and air-conditioning company. He never really gave much thought to being any-thing other than a draftsman.

That changed when he went with his wife on a business-related golf trip. It was sponsored by a radio station where his wife's company did some advertising. The usual small talk ensued with various employees from the radio broadcasting station. However, when he started talking with a couple of the broadcasters, they were surprised to discover that Cordova was a draftsman. Apparently, Cordova has the out-going, "never met a stranger" personality of a natural-born salesperson. They just couldn't picture him quietly sitting at a drawing board all day.

For some reason, this bothered these guys so much that when they got back to the office they called and asked him to come in for an interview. They needed someone with a sports background to handle some special advertising accounts involving the California Angels and Los Angeles Rams for one of their radio stations.

Cordova had played sports in college and was a huge sports fan. That and his winning personality landed him a fun new job in radio ad sales.

MORE TWISTS AND TURNS

This sweet little deal went on for a couple of years until the owner of the station, Bob Bingham, sold the station. Cordova really enjoyed working for Bingham, but he really didn't enjoy working for the new station owner, so he quit and went back to drafting. Big mistake! After drafting what seemed like the millionth blueprint, drafting just didn't do it for Cordova anymore. So when Mr. Bingham called a couple years later to offer him an opportunity to handle the franchise sales for new international company he'd started, Cordova was more than happy to accept.

Now Cordova works for a company called Little Gym International, the number-one motor skills development pro-gram in the world. Essentially, Little Gyms are a place for tots (ages one to six) to work out in a playful, noncompetitive environment.

BACK WHERE HE BELONGS

Cordova says that one of the reasons he enjoys his work so much is that he really believes in the product he sells. He says the world of children's sports and fitness has gotten so high pressure that kids are pushed to win and be the best. He appreciates the Little Gym approach, which lets kids be kids without fearing failure.

Cordova says his product is so good that the franchises pretty much sell themselves. He never makes cold calls. Instead, Little Gym International uses the Internet, its own website, word-of-mouth recommendations from impressed customers, and its solid reputation to bring in new business. Cordova isn't the only person who thinks the Little Gym franchise is great. The company makes regular appearances on *Entrepreneur* magazine's list of top franchises and is known as one of the fastest-growing franchise companies around. Little Gyms are popping up all over the country and the world. France and Puerto Rico are recent additions to the international Little Gym family.

ONE-WAY TICKET

Cordova says that education is your ticket to success. However, education can only get your foot in the door. Your performance is what counts after that. He says it's important to enjoy what you're doing. That way you'll be glad to do a good job. He knows the difference between sticking it out in a job that doesn't fit and flourishing in a job that fits like a glove.

Textile Manufacturer

SHORTCUTS

GO visit a fabric store and compare all the different kinds of textiles you find there.

READ some favorite fairy tales and pay attention to see how textiles are woven into the story. For links to stories such as "The Emperor's New Clothes," "Rumpelstilzchen," "Sleeping Beauty," and "Rapunzel," go to http://www.capcollege.bc.ca/dept/textile/fairytale.html.

TRY working on a variety of arts and crafts projects using textiles. You'll find instructions and loads of interesting information at the Textile Discovery Space at http://www.hiraeth.com/ytg/welcome.htm.

SKILL SET

✔ ART

✔ SCIENCE

✔ MONEY

WHAT IS A TEXTILE MANUFACTURER?

In the old days, people spun and wove the cloth they need-ed to make clothes. Then came Eli Whitney's cotton gin and the Industrial Revolution, and things have never been the same since. Now textile manufacturing is an incredibly sophisticated process that results in an amazing array of nat-ural and synthetic fibers. These fibers are used to make the clothes people wear, the fabrics they decorate their homes and furniture with, the fabricated parts in automobiles and airplanes (such as seats), protective gear used by law enforce-ment officers, materials used to make roads, and even the materials used to keep astronauts safe in space.

Textile manufacturers are the people who oversee the details in the textile industry. Part scientist, part engineer, and part manager, a textile manufacturer is responsible for figuring out the best ways to produce a particular kind of fiber and then making sure it gets produced efficiently. Computers and other technology make it possible to do things Eli Whitney could have never imagined. It's challenging work and it pays well for the specialized skills a well-trained textile manufacturer brings to the job.

There are a number of exceptional textile programs offered in colleges across the country. Most textile programs offer a variety of specialties including textile chemistry—the chemical and industrial processes involved in the production of all kinds of fibers. Another area of textile opportunity is textile technology, which includes textile design, manufacturing management, quality assurance, and new product development. Other opportunities in this industry are found in textile engineering. Textile engineers design and make products, machinery, and manufacturing systems that are used to keep the textile industry running smoothly.

The textile industry is huge. It generates more than $70 billion of the U.S. gross national product each year and accounts for about 20 percent of the entire world trade. But manufacturing is just one of the many ways to make textiles a part of your career. There are also opportunities in design and color, sales and marketing, and research and development. In addition, there are some interesting ways to add an international flair to your profession;

there are increasing opportunities in managing and coordinating resources for textile products and in finding markets for products all over the world.

Sometimes careers in textiles are so obvious that they get overlooked. There are fashion designers, clothing manufacturers, fashion merchandisers, fashion buyers, pattern makers, cutters, and machinists. People take for granted that stores will always have clothes to buy without thinking about the amazing processes that got those clothes there in the first place. Here's your chance to weave a future in textiles.

TRY IT OUT

FEELING GOOD

The way a textile feels to the touch is called its "hand." Different types of fabric have different types of "hands." For instance, the "hand" of the denim in your jeans is different from the "hand" of your T-shirt—even though both fabrics are made from the same fiber: cotton.

You can get a good feel for the types of fabrics produced by the textile industry by visiting a fabric or sewing goods store. Ask if you can have (or purchase) small samples of a variety of different fabrics and use them to start your own fabric scrapbook. Attach each sample to a separate sheet of paper and write notes about anything you can learn about them—the ingredients, the care instructions, the manufacturing process, etc.

VIRTUAL TOURS

Thanks to the wonders of the Internet, you can explore textile museums all over the world right from the comfort of your home. Some on-line tours you won't want to miss include:

- The Museum of Textiles in Toronto, Ontario, at http://www.museumfortextiles.on.ca
- Victoria and Albert Museum in London, England, at http://www.vam.uk/collections/collections/text_dress.htm

☿ The Textiles Room at http://www.texnet.it/tessile. ttrmus

☿ Fine Art Museum of San Francisco at http://www. thinker.org/deyoung/collections/textiles.html

☿ Cooper Hewitt Museum of the Smithsonian Institution at http://www.si.edu/ndm

☿ Shetland Museum in Shetland, United Kingdom, at http://www.shetlandmuseum.org.uk/museum

☿ The Textile Museum in Washington, D.C., at http:// www.textilemuseum.org

Keep track of each site that you visit. Which did you like the most?

READ ALL ABOUT IT
Find out about all kinds of opportunities involving textiles and the fashion industry in the following resources:

Black, Judy. *Now Hiring: Fashion.* New York: Silver Burdett Press, 1994.

Burns, Leslie Davis, and Nancy O'Bryant. *The Business of Fashion: Designing, Manufacturing, and Marketing.* New York: Fairchild Publications, 1998.

Giacobello, John. *Careers in the Fashion Industry.* New York: Rosen Publishing Group, 1999.

Jarnow, Jeanette A., and Bradley J. Potthoff. *Inside the Fashion Business.* New York: Simon & Schuster, 1996.

Johnson, Maurice J., and Evelyn C. Moore. *So You Want to Work in the Fashion Business?: A Practical Look at Apparel Product Development and Global Manufacturing.* Upper Saddle River, N.J.: Prentice-Hall, 1997.

Mauro, Lucia. *Careers for Fashion Plates and Other Trendsetters.* Lincolnwood, Ill.: NTC Publishing Group, 1996.

EVERYTHING YOU WANTED TO KNOW ABOUT TEXTILES
If you get to visit only one textile-related website, make it http://www.fabrics.com. Here you'll find absolutely every-

thing you could possibly want to know about textiles, including apparel fabric, automotive fabric, industrial fabric, and medical fabric.

Just for fun, click on the fabric terms icon and hop over to the "fabric-isms" page. See if you can add to their list of sayings, movies, and songs that contain fabric terms.

JUST IN CASE YOU MISSED SOMETHING

Still looking for interesting information about textiles? Try some of these websites:

Textile Industry Affair at http://www.textileaffairs.com

Textile Exchange at http://www.international-textile-exchange.com

A COLORFUL CAREER

Color plays an important role in the textile industry. Start noticing how color affects your life. Look around your class and see if you can tell what the "hot" new colors are. Visit a furniture store and see if you can tell what the "in" colors are for home decoration. Notice how different colors look together. You may even want to get out your old box of Crayolas and experiment with different color combinations. See if you can mix the colors to invent a brand-new color.

For more technical information about color, take a look at some of the following websites:

- ☼ Color Matters includes starting points for how color affects people's minds, their behavior, and the world around them. Find it all at http://www.colormatters.com.
- ☼ The Color Association of the United States is the source for each season's winning colors. Get the scoop and find out about some interesting resources at http://www.colorassociation.com.

CHECK IT OUT

American Textile Manufacturers Institute
1130 Connecticut Avenue NW, Suite 1200
Washington, D.C. 20036-0500
http://www.atmi.org

The Cotton Foundation
P.O. Box 820284
Memphis, Tennessee 38182-0284
http://www.cotton.org

Industrial Fabrics Association International
1801 County Road B West
Roseville, Minn. 55113-4061
http://www.ifai.com

Institute of Textile Technology
2551 Ivy Road
Charlottesville, Virginia 22903
http://www.itt.edu

GET ACQUAINTED

Jennifer Hrometz,
Textile Manufacturer

CAREER PATH

CHILDHOOD ASPIRATION: To be a lawyer (as encouraged by her parents, who were impressed with her ability to debate anything).

FIRST JOB: Mowing lawns for $5 each.

CURRENT JOB: Director of Design for Chatham Textiles.

OFF TO AN EARLY START

When Jennifer Hrometz was a kid, she'd never heard of the textile industry. She had no idea that all the time she spent coloring in her coloring books and painting with her paint-by-numbers kits was giving her some good training for a great career. Looking back, Hrometz says that some of the skills that help her most on the job are the ones that just came naturally to her. The school she attended was too small to offer formal art training, but Hrometz says her teachers must have recognized her artistic talent because they were always asking her to help decorate the classroom bulletin boards.

She says she must have had some natural leadership ability too because she was the one they always asked to be in charge when they had to leave the room for a few minutes. Hrometz says these experiences helped build her confidence and prepare her for the work she does now.

WEAVING A FUTURE

Hrometz had never considered a career in textiles until two recruiters from North Carolina State University's textile school came to visit her high school. Through them, she discovered a career path that combined creativity and technology: textile design. Hrometz credits the support she received from several of her professors for helping her figure out how to best put her talents to use in the textile industry.

YOU CALL THIS WORK?

Finding a good job after graduation was a breeze for Hrometz. Her newfound skills were in big demand. She started her textile career as a textile designer and has worked her way up to direct the entire design and development staffs at her company.

Hrometz says she feels lucky to have discovered this profession. She loves her job and is excited about going to work every day. Her company manufactures fabrics for furniture companies all over the world, which means that Hrometz's job takes her all over the world to places like Belgium, Italy,

New York, and San Francisco. She travels to meet with clients, to research industry trends, and to attend "trunk shows" where she helps showcase her company's products.

A COLORFUL CAREER

One of the best parts of Hrometz's job is creating new colors. Twice a year, she gets together with 600 to 700 other color designers to decide what the "hot" new colors are for home furnishings, wall covering, carpet, and apparel.

New colors come about through lots of research, involving consumer interests as well as economic, ergonomic, and environmental factors. Hrometz recently discovered a wonderful new color in Belgium called "mink." Mink has purple chocolate tones and looks great with olive green and fuchsia.

WAY TO GO

Pushing the envelope is what makes the company Hrometz works for and its fabrics stand out from the competition. She says her willingness to find ways to do what "can't be done" has paid off in big ways for her company. In one instance, she worked night and day (and weekends too!) to perfect a new type of thread. Her persistence paid off with the launch of 24 colors in a new fabric line called Lancaster. The fabric line was eventually "placed" (textile industry lingo for being purchased for use by various clients) by big-name companies all over the world. It remains one of Hrometz's employer's top sellers and is credited with being the trigger to $10,000,000 worth of sales in just 18 months—a record for the company.

DON'T WORK FOR A LIVING

Hrometz believes that if you do what you love, the money will follow. When you find work that you love to do, it doesn't seem like work. Instead, you find the passion you need to stay focused, ride the ups and downs of any career, and keep a positive attitude. According to Hrometz, the best career move you can make is to pick something that you really enjoy.

Venture Capitalist

SHORTCUTS

GO on-line to see *American Venture Magazine* at http://www.avce.com. It includes all kinds of information for venture capitalists.

READ the business pages of your local newspaper to find out about up-and-coming businesses.

TRY out the stock market. Stein Roe Young Investors has a mutual fund just for kids. To order a very informative educational packet, call toll-free 1-800-403-KIDS.

SKILL SET

✔ MONEY

✔ ADVENTURE

✔ COMPUTERS

WHAT IS A VENTURE CAPITALIST?

Venture capitalists invest money in promising new or growing businesses in the hopes of making more money—sooner rather than later. Three to seven years is the typical time span between payout and payoff on a venture capital project.

Venture capital arrangements are not new. One of the first known "venture capitalists" was named Isabella. She was a Spanish queen who put her money behind a certain explorer named Christopher Columbus. Needless to say, the results of this arrangement got the venture capital business off to an interesting start.

Nowadays, venture capitalists are still funding great adventures into uncharted territories. Instead of crossing oceans and discovering new lands, however, the discoveries made possible by venture capitalists are more likely to involve information technology, biotechnology, telecommunications, and useful new inventions. Can you imagine being there at the start of fledgling companies that later became Microsoft, FedEx, and Intel? It was venture capital that brought such innovation and technology into the mainstream of the business world.

Although you may not hear as much about these types of deals in the news, venture capitalists are also often behind projects involving construction, industrial products, and all kinds of business services. In fact, just follow the money behind any big, financially risky project, and you're likely to find a venture capitalist.

In exchange for their investment, venture capitalists generally get 30 to 50 percent ownership of the business. However, money isn't the only thing that many venture capitalists invest in these businesses. They also protect their investments by providing management expertise and other kinds of help to guide start-up companies to success.

Even though venture capital investments almost always involve lots of money—a minimum of $1 million to $2 million dollars by some accounts—the money doesn't necessarily come from the venture capitalists' own pockets. Sure, there are some wealthy individuals who use their own money to

fund these types of investments. But venture capitalists are just as likely to be extremely capable business professionals who use money from a fund put together by a group of wealthy investors, a bank, or a corporation.

Regardless of where the money comes from, venture capitalists are trained to recognize a winner. They are always on the lookout for new or growing businesses on the verge of big success. They review hundreds of business plans to find a handful that show real promise. From this handful, venture capitalists begin a process called "due diligence," which involves some very complicated research into the viability of an idea, the credibility of the people involved in the business itself, and the possibilities for success. After all this work is done, the eventual decisions, be they good or bad, are pretty much determined by gut instincts.

How does someone get the kind of good business instincts that others will trust with millions, and sometimes even billions, of dollars? Education, experience, and lots of it. A typical route to a venture capital firm starts in a good business school, earning a degree in business, finance, or economics. Next comes work experience in business, banking, or the stock market. Some people get their start working in a venture capital firm—doing anything that needs to get done and working their way up from the bottom. Any way you go, you'll need to understand how business works, the ins and outs of the stock market and other types of investing, and how to get along with the movers and shakers of the business world.

Even with the best ingredients—plenty of money, great ideas and products, and a sound management team—industry statistics indicate that up to one-third of these investments fail altogether and never pay out a dime and another third will just break even. What keeps this industry going is the final one-third, which are ventures that end up very successful and return 8 to 10 times the original investment.

Venture capital isn't a "get rich quick" sort of scheme. It's a sophisticated business run by adventurous businesspeople who aren't afraid to take a gamble on the future. It isn't for everyone. Fortunes are made—and lost—in this business.

TRY IT OUT

THE MONEY GAME

Money makes the venture capital world go round. And much of that money is made (and sometimes lost) on Wall Street. Study how the stock market works, and you'll learn quite a bit about how the venture capital game is played. Here are a few easy and even fun ways to start the process:

- ☿ Edustock at http://www.thinkquest.org/3088/ welcome/welcome.html is a good place to start learning about the stock market. It includes tutorials on the stock market and how to pick good stocks.
- ☿ E*Trade at http://game.etrade.com offers the chance to play a very realistic virtual version of the stock market. It's make-believe money you use for buying and selling fictional stock, but you can win real prizes if you beat the odds—and the other players.
- ☿ Another stock market simulation can be found at http://www.sandbox.net/finalbell/pub-bin/page?fb_ptm_main+main.html. This site gives you a chance to practice your on-line investing skills and strategies while competing for daily "sand dollars" and other great prizes.
- ☿ Sign up at http://investorsleague.com to play the free nVestor stock simulation game, and you'll receive a $100,000 in a virtual stock portfolio.

SHOW ME THE MONEY

If you hope to someday manage lots of money, learn to manage the little bit you have now. Here are some helpful resources to get you going.

Godfrey, Neale S. *Ultimate Kids' Money Book.* New York: Simon & Schuster, 1998.

Karlitz, Gail, and Debbie Honig. *Growing Money: A Complete Investing Guide for Kids.* New York: Price Stern Sloan, 1999.

McAleese, Tama. *Money: How to Get It, Keep It, Make It Grow.* New York: Chelsea House Publishing, 1997.

Otkinoski, Steve. *The Kid's Guide to Money: Earning It, Saving It, Spending It, Growing It, Sharing It.* New York: Scholastic, 1996.

TAKE YOUR PICK

Visit some of the websites frequented by venture capitalists who are looking to help promising start-up businesses. Find out what kinds of companies attract the big bucks. Interesting sites to peruse include:

- http://www.garage.com
- http://www.vcapital.com
- http://www.venture-capitalist.com
- http://www.venturepreneurs.com

If you had a couple million bucks to invest, where would you put it? What types of businesses sound good to you? Internet start-ups? A new invention? Medical technology?

IT'S ALL IN THE PLAN

Write a business plan now so you'll recognize a good one later. You'll find free templates and lots of tips at the following websites:

http://www.vfinance.com (You'll also find ads for real businesses that are up for sale at this site.)

http://www.nvst.com (More good stuff for aspiring venture capitalists and entrepreneurs alike.)

Who knows? Maybe instead of becoming a venture capitalist, you'll need one to fund your hot new start-up company!

BEHIND THE MONEY

Recent years have brought incredible success stories involving venture capital projects, especially in an area called

Silicon Valley in California. Here's where you find amazing computer and technology companies all trying to come up with the latest and greatest new twist on technology. Use an Internet browser to see what you can find out about this hotbed of innovation.

CHECK IT OUT

National Association for Small Business Investment Companies
666 11th Street NW, Suite 750
Washington, D.C. 20001
http://www.nasbic.org

National Venture Capital Association
1655 N. Fort Myer Drive, Suite 850
Arlington, Virginia 22209
http://www.nvca.org

GET ACQUAINTED

Bill Elsner,
Venture Capitalist

CAREER PATH

CHILDHOOD ASPIRATION: To be a ski instructor.

FIRST JOB: Made the rounds as a young boy delivering papers, mowing lawns, and shoveling snow.

CURRENT JOB: Partner, Telecom Partners, a venture capital firm.

A ROUNDABOUT ROUTE

Bill Elsner never intended to become a venture capitalist. After trying several different majors in college, he finally settled on accounting because it would provide a good background for getting into law school. His original plan was to graduate, make a little money as an accountant, go back to law school, and become a lawyer.

But plans often change. After graduating, Elsner landed a good job as an accountant with one of the "big eight" accounting firms, and he discovered he actually liked accounting. So he forgot about law school. He became a CPA (certified public accountant) and stayed with the firm for six years.

At that point, one of Elsner's clients lured him away from the accounting firm to serve as chief financial officer for a publicly traded cable and telecommunications company. This was another good move, one Elsner enjoyed until he decided to start his own cable company specializing in international projects.

After building a thriving company that was doing business in 22 countries, Elsner took it public in an initial public offering (IPO)—for a tidy profit, of course. He stayed on to help run the company for a few years and started dabbling in the venture capital game. He invested his own money in a couple of start-up companies and, when he saw a return, liked what happened.

So when the opportunity presented itself to join forces with a partner who had started a venture capital firm by raising $15 million from a number of wealthy individuals, it was easy for Elsner to say yes. Elsner's partner had launched the company with a fund called Telecom Partners I. Together they started a second phase of the fund, called Telecom Partners II, and pulled together $125 million from influential partners such as the Massachusetts Institute of Technology (MIT) and the Howard Hughes Medical Fund. Phase three of the fund, Telecom Partners III, brought in $500 million for new projects. By then, Elsner was a full-fledged venture capitalist by anyone's definition.

THE CASE OF THE SERIAL ENTREPRENEURS

Venture capitalist or not, Elsner discovered he was still an entrepreneur at heart. So he and his partner run their firm a little differently than other venture capitalists. Instead of seeking out innovative companies that other people want to start, they start their own new companies. All their companies are very specialized with in the telecommunications industry.

Elsner and his partner spot a good idea, scout it out, and if it looks promising enough, put a management team in place to make a go of it. For example, Elsner discovered that in Brazil there were only 10 telephone lines per 100 people. (Compare that to 75 telephone lines per 100 people in the United States.) Elsner had a hunch that there might be a business opportunity waiting for someone who could find a way to offer alternative phone service at a lower cost. He and his partner made half a dozen trips to Brazil to investigate the situation. They ended up obtaining licenses to cover three-quarters of the country with wireless phone service. That hunch continues to pay off in a big way.

SECRETS OF SUCCESS

There are a few things Elsner would like you to know about choosing a career and making money.

1. **Money isn't everything.** Sure, it takes money to launch a business, but Elsner says that the key to success is not in the dollars but in the people. A great idea with a mediocre management team is doomed to fail. A so-so idea with a great management team will thrive. It's the quality of the people, not the quantity of dollars, that makes the difference.

2. **Money isn't everything.** Even if you make a million bucks, your career won't be worth much if you aren't enjoying yourself. From his high school days working at a ski resort and his college summers spent as a lifeguard, Elsner learned that work can be fun. Looking

forward to going to work every day is much more important to him than making lots of money.

3. **Money isn't everything.** Elsner urges anyone who is planning to make money the focal point of his or her career to reconsider. He says you'll find more success if you figure out what you're good at and then do a good job. The quality of your work will take you places you never thought possible.

MAKE A DETOUR THAT PAYS OFF!

Follow the money to more interesting career options. Make sure to find work you really enjoy, something you believe in, and something that will make you glad to get out of bed each morning. Find your passion and let it lead you to your future—and your fortune.

Go through these lists of suggested careers and see if some sound right for you. If you're not familiar with one of them, or if one (or more!) sounds particularly intriguing, look it up in one of the career encyclopedias listed on page 178.

If the future is anything like the present, information is where it's at. There is lots of opportunity for salaries at the high end as well as plenty of ways to spin off a new entrepreneurial venture with a technological twist.

THE BUCK STOPS HERE

CAREERS THAT COMPUTE

analyst
computer consultant
computer security analyst
data communications analyst
database administrator
information systems
   developer
information systems
   manager
information technology
   manager
internet developer

LAN (local area network)
   manager
network administrator
on-line services manager
operating systems
   programmer
operations manager
programmer
software support technician
software tester
systems analyst
webmaster

CASH IN ON THE INTERNET

The past few years have brought an explosion of new opportunities on the World Wide Web. Most of the jobs listed here weren't even invented 5 or 10 years ago. Who knows what kinds of "cyber" jobs there will be when you get ready to start your career.

computer consultant
cyber security specialist
intranet network administrator

network administrator
webmaster
website programmer

WORKING FOR THE BIG PAYOFF

According to the U.S. Bureau of Labor Statistics, the top-paying jobs in United States are (in order of income potential):

physicians and surgeons
dentists
podiatrists
petroleum engineers
aircraft pilots and flight
  engineers
lawyers
engineering, math, and
  natural science managers
optometrists
physicists and astronomers
aeronautical engineers and
  astronautical engineers
actuaries
pharmacists
computer engineers

chemical engineers
chiropractors
education administrators
farm and home management
  advisers
electrical and electronic
  engineers
general managers and top
  executives
medical scientists
physical therapists
nuclear engineers
industrial engineers
mining engineers
financial managers

BANKING ON A CAREER IN MONEY

Want to make good money for your work? The financial world is a good place to be.

auditor
benefits officer
certified financial analyst
commercial banker
commodities broker
commodities risk manager
corporate financial analyst
credit manager
financial planner
foreign exchange
  representative

investment analyst
investment manager
investor relations officer
loan officer
market maker
mortgage broker
mutual fund manager
securities analyst
stockbroker

INFORMATION IS POWER

Mind-boggling, isn't it? There are so many great choices, so many jobs you've never heard of before. How will you ever narrow it down to the perfect spot for you?

First, pinpoint the ideas that sound the most interesting to you. Then, find out all you can about them. As you may have noticed, a similar pattern of information was used for each of the career entries featured in this book. Each entry included

💡 a general description or definition of the career
💡 some hands-on projects that give readers a chance to actually experience a job
💡 a list of organizations to contact for more information
💡 an interview with a professional

You can use information like this to help you determine the best career path to pursue. Since there isn't room in one book to profile all these money-related career choices, here's your chance to do it yourself. Conduct a full investigation into a financial career that interests you.

Please Note: If this book does not belong to you, use a separate sheet of paper to record your responses to the following questions.

CAREER TITLE _____

WHAT IS A _____?
Use career encyclopedias and other resources to write a description of this career.

SKILL SET
✔ _____
✔ _____
✔ _____

TRY IT OUT
Write project ideas here. Ask your parents and your teacher to come up with a plan.

CHECK IT OUT
List professional organizations where you can learn more about this profession.

GET ACQUAINTED
Interview a professional in the field and summarize your findings.

DON'T STOP NOW!

GO FOR IT!

It's been a fast-paced trip so far. Take a break, regroup, and look at all the progress you've made.

1st Stop: Self-Discovery
You discovered some personal interests and natural abilities that you can start building a career around.

2nd Stop: Exploration
You've explored an exciting array of career opportunities with money. You're now aware that your career can involve either a specialized area with many educational requirements or that it can involve a practical application of skills with a minimum of training and experience.

At this point, you've found a couple of (or few) careers that really intrigue you. Now it's time to put it all together and do all you can to make an informed, intelligent choice. It's time to move on.

3rd Stop: Experimentation

By the time you finish this section, you'll have reached one of three points in the career planning process.

1. **Green light!** You found it. No need to look any further. This is *the* career for you. (This may happen to a lucky few. Don't worry if it hasn't happened yet for you. This whole process is about exploring options, experimenting with ideas, and, eventually, making the best choice for you.)

2. **Yellow light!** Close, but not quite. You seem to be on the right path but you haven't nailed things down for sure. (This is where many people your age end up, and it's a good place to be. You've learned what it takes to really check things out. Hang in there. Your time will come.)

3. **Red light!** Whoa! No doubt about it, this career just isn't for you. (Congratulations! Aren't you glad you found out now and not after you'd spent four years in college preparing for this career? Your next stop: Make a U-turn and start this process over with another career.)

Here's a sneak peek at what you'll be doing in the next section.

☼ First, you'll pick a favorite career idea (or two or three).

☼ Second, you'll snoop around the library to find answers to the 10 things you've just got to know about your future career.

☼ Third, you'll pick up the phone and talk to someone whose career you admire to find out what it's really like.

☼ Fourth, you'll link up with a whole world of great information about your career idea on the Internet (it's easier than you think).

☼ Fifth, you'll go on the job to shadow a professional for a day.

Hang on to your hats and get ready to make tracks!

#1 NARROW DOWN YOUR CHOICES

You've been introduced to quite a few money-related career ideas. You may also have some ideas of your own to add. Which ones appeal to you the most?

Write your top three choices in the spaces below. (Sorry if this is starting to sound like a broken record, but . . . **if this book does not belong to you, write your responses on a separate sheet of paper.**)

1.
2.
3.

WRITE YOUR RESPONSES ON A SEPARATE PIECE OF PAPER

#2 SNOOP AT THE LIBRARY

Take your list of favorite career ideas, a notebook, and a helpful adult with you to the library. When you get there, go to the reference section and ask the librarian to help you find

books about careers. Most libraries will have at least one set of career encyclopedias. Some of the larger libraries may also have career information on CD-ROM.

Gather all the information you can and use it to answer the following questions in your notebook about each of the careers on your list. Make sure to ask for help if you get stuck.

TOP 10 THINGS YOU NEED TO KNOW ABOUT YOUR CAREER

1. What kinds of skills does this job require?
2. What kind of training is required? (Compare the options for a high school degree, trade school degree, two-year degree, four-year degree, and advanced degree.)
3. What types of classes do I need to take in high school in order to be accepted into a training program?
4. What are the names of three schools or colleges where I can get the training I need?
5. Are there any apprenticeship or internship opportunities available? If so, where? If not, could I create my own opportunity? How?
6. How much money can I expect to earn as a beginner? How much with more experience?
7. What kinds of places hire people to do this kind of work?
8. What is a typical work environment like? For example, would I work in a busy office, outdoors, or in a laboratory?
9. What are some books and magazines I could read to learn more about this career? Make a list and look for them at your library.
10. Where can I write for more information? Make a list of professional associations.

#3 CHAT ON THE PHONE

Talking to a seasoned professional—someone who experiences the job day in and day out—can be a great way to get the inside story on what a career is all about. Fortunately for you, the experts in any career field can be as close as the nearest telephone.

Sure it can be a bit scary calling up an adult whom you don't know. But, two things are in your favor:

1. They can't see you. The worst thing they can do is hang up on you, so just relax and enjoy the conversation.
2. They'll probably be happy to talk to you about their job. In fact, most people will be flattered that you've called. If you happen to contact someone who seems reluctant to talk, thank them for their time and try someone else.

Here are a few pointers to help make your telephone interview a success.

☼ Mind your manners and speak clearly.
☼ Be respectful of their time and position.
☼ Be prepared with good questions and take notes as you talk.

One more commonsense reminder: Be careful about giving out your address and DO NOT arrange to meet anyone you don't know without your parents' supervision.

TRACKING DOWN CAREER EXPERTS

You might be wondering by now how to find someone to interview. Have no fear! It's easy, if you're persistent. All you have to do is ask. Ask the right people and you'll have a great lead in no time.

A few of the people to ask and sources to turn to are

Your parents. They may know someone (or know someone who knows someone) who has just the kind of job you're looking for.

Your friends and neighbors. You might be surprised to find out how many interesting jobs these people have when you start asking them what they (or their parents) do for a living.

Librarians. Since you've already figured out what kinds of companies employ people in your field of interest, the next step is to ask for information about local employers. Although it's a bit cumbersome to use, a big volume called *Contacts Influential* can provide this kind of information.

Professional associations. Call or write to the professional associations you discovered in Activity #1 a few pages back and ask for recommendations.

Chambers of commerce. The local chamber of commerce probably has a directory of employers, their specialties, and their phone numbers. Call the chamber, explain what you are looking for, and give the person a chance to help the future workforce.

Newspaper and magazine articles. Find an article about the subject you are interested in. Chances are pretty good that it will mention the name of at least one expert in the field. The article probably won't include the person's phone number (that would be too easy), so you'll have to look for clues. Common clues include the name of the company that the expert works for, the town that he or she lives in, and if the person is an author, the name of his or her publisher. Make a few phone calls and track the person down (if long distance calls are involved, make sure to get your parents' permission first).

INQUIRING KIDS WANT TO KNOW

Before you make the call, make a list of questions to ask. You'll cover more ground if you focus on using the five w's (and the h) that you've probably heard about in your creative writing classes: Who? What? Where? When? How? and Why? For example,

1. Who do you work for?
2. What is a typical work day like for you?
3. Where can I get some on-the-job experience?
4. When did you become a _____ ?
   (profession)
5. How much can you earn in this profession? (But, remember it's not polite to ask someone how much *he* or *she* earns.)
6. Why did you choose this profession?

One last suggestion: Add a professional (and very classy) touch to the interview process by following up with a thank-you note to the person who took time out of a busy schedule to talk with you.

#4 SURF THE NET

With the Internet, the new information superhighway, charging full steam ahead, you literally have a world of information at your fingertips. The Internet has something for everyone, and it's getting easier to access all the time. An increasing number of libraries and schools are

offering access to the Internet on their computers. In addition, companies such as America Online and CompuServe have made it possible for anyone with a home computer to surf the World Wide Web.

A typical career search will land everything from the latest news on developments in the field and course notes from universities to museum exhibits, interactive games, educational activities, and more. You just can't beat the timeliness or the variety of information available on the Net.

One of the easiest ways to track down this information is to use an Internet search engine, such as Yahoo! Simply type in the topic you are looking for, and in a matter of seconds, you'll have a list of options from around the world. It's fun to browse—you never know what you'll come up with.

To narrow down your search a bit, look for specific web-sites, forums, or chatrooms that are related to your topic in the following publications:

Hahn, Harley. *Harley Hahn's Internet and Web Yellow Pages.* Berkeley, Calif.: Osborne McGraw-Hill, 1999.

Polly, Jean Armour. *The Internet Kids and Family Yellow Pages.* Berkeley, Calif.: Osborne McGraw-Hill, 1999.

Turner, Marcia Layton, and Audrey Seybold. *Official World Wide Web Yellow Pages.* Indianapolis: Que, 1999.

To go on-line at home you may want to compare two of the more popular on-line services: America Online and CompuServe. Please note that there is a monthly subscription fee for using these services. There can also be extra fees attached to specific forums and services, so *make sure you have your parents' OK before you sign up.* For information about America Online call 800-827-6364. For information about CompuServe call 800-848-8990. Both services frequently offer free start-up deals, so shop around.

There are also many other services, depending on where you live. Check your local phone book or ads in local computer magazines for other service options.

Before you link up, keep in mind that many of these sites are geared toward professionals who are already working in a particular field. Some of the sites can get pretty technical. Just use the experience as a chance to nose around the field, hang out with the people who are tops in the field, and think about whether or not you'd like to be involved in a profession like that.

Specific sites to look for are the following:

Professional associations. Find out about what's happening in the field, conferences, journals, and other helpful tidbits.

Schools that specialize in this area. Many include research tools, introductory courses, and all kinds of interesting information.

Government agencies. Quite a few are going high-tech with lots of helpful resources.

Websites hosted by experts in the field (this seems to be a popular hobby among many professionals). These websites are often as entertaining as they are informative.

If you're not sure where to go, just start clicking around. Sites often link to other sites. You may want to jot down notes about favorite sites. Sometimes you can even print out information that isn't copyright-protected; try the print option and see what happens.

Be prepared: Surfing the Internet can be an addicting habit! There is so much great information. It's a fun way to focus on your future.

#5 SHADOW A PROFESSIONAL

Linking up with someone who is gainfully employed in a profession that you want to explore is a great way to find out what a career is like. Following someone around while the person are at work is called "shadowing." Try it!

This process involves three steps.

1. Find someone to shadow. Some suggestions include
   - ☿ the person you interviewed (if you enjoyed talking with him or her and feel comfortable about asking the person to show you around the workplace)
   - ☿ friends and neighbors (you may even be shocked to discover that your parents have interesting jobs)
   - ☿ workers at the chamber of commerce may know of mentoring programs available in your area (it's a popular concept, so most larger areas should have something going on)
   - ☿ someone at your local School-to-Work office, the local Boy Scouts Explorer program director (this is available to girls too!), or your school guidance counselor
2. Make a date. Call and make an appointment. Find out when is the best time for arrival and departure. Make arrangements with a parent or other respected adult to go with you and get there on time.
3. Keep your ears and eyes open. This is one time when it is OK to be nosy. Ask

questions. Notice everything that is happening around you. Ask your host to let you try some of the tasks he or she is doing.

The basic idea of the shadowing experience is to put yourself in the other person's shoes and see how they fit. Imagine yourself having a job like this 10 or 15 years down the road. It's a great way to find out if you are suited for a particular line of work.

BE CAREFUL OUT THERE!

Two cautions must accompany this recommendation. First, remember the stranger danger rules of your childhood. NEVER meet with anyone you don't know without your parents' permission and ALWAYS meet in a supervised situation—at the office or with your parents.

Second, be careful not to overdo it. These people are busy earning a living, so respect their time by limiting your contact and coming prepared with valid questions and background information.

PLAN B

If shadowing opportunities are limited where you live, try one of these approaches for learning the ropes from a professional.

Pen pals. Find a mentor who is willing to share information, send interesting materials, or answer specific questions that come up during your search.

Cyber pals. Go on-line in a forum or chatroom related to your profession. You'll be able to chat with professionals from all over the world.

If you want to get some more on-the-job experience, try one of these approaches.

Volunteer to do the dirty work. Volunteer to work for someone who has a job that interests you for a specified period of time. Do anything—filing, errands, emptying trash cans—that puts you in contact with professionals. Notice every tiny detail about the profession. Listen to the lingo they use in the profession. Watch how they perform their jobs on a day-to-day basis.

Be an apprentice. This centuries-old job training method is making a comeback. Find out if you can set up an official on-the-job training program to gain valuable experience. Ask professional associations about apprenticeship opportunities. Once again, a School-to-Work program can be a great asset. In many areas, they've established some very interesting career training opportunities.

Hire yourself for the job. Maybe you are simply too young to do much in the way of on-the-job training right now. That's OK. Start learning all you can now and you'll be ready to really wow them when the time is right. Make sure you do all the Try It Out activities included for the career(s) you are most interested in. Use those activities as a starting point for creating other projects that will give you a feel for what the job is like.

WHAT'S NEXT?

Have you carefully worked your way through all of the suggested activities? You haven't tried to sneak past anything, have you? This isn't a place for shortcuts. If you've done the activities, you're ready to decide where you stand with each career idea. So what is it? Green light? See page 170. Yellow light? See page 169. Red light? See page 168. Find the spot that best describes your response to what you've discovered about this career idea and plan your next move.

RED LIGHT

So you've decided this career is definitely not for you—hang in there! The process of elimination is an important one. You've learned some valuable career planning skills; use them to explore other ideas. In the meantime, use the following road map to chart a plan to get beyond this "spinning your wheels" point in the process.

Take a variety of classes at school to expose yourself to new ideas and expand the options. Make a list of courses you want to try.

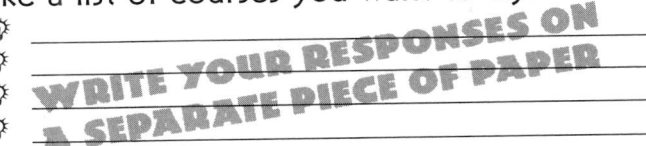

- 💡 _____
- 💡 _____
- 💡 _____
- 💡 _____

Get involved in clubs and other after-school activities (like 4-H or Boy Scout Explorers) to further develop your interests. Write down some that interest you.

- 💡 _____
- 💡 _____
- 💡 _____
- 💡 _____

Read all you can find about interesting people and their work. Make a list of people you'd like to learn more about.

- 💡 _____
- 💡 _____
- 💡 _____
- 💡 _____

Keep at it. Time is on your side. Finding the perfect work for you is worth a little effort. Once you've crossed this hurdle, move on to the next pages and continue mapping out a great future.

YELLOW LIGHT

Proceed with caution. While the idea continues to intrigue you, you may wonder if it's the best choice for you. Your concerns are legitimate (listen to that nagging little voice inside!).

Maybe it's the training requirements that intimidate you. Maybe you have concerns about finding a good job once you complete the training. Maybe you wonder if you have what it takes to do the job.

At this point, it's good to remember that there is often more than one way to get somewhere. Check out all the choices and choose the route that's best for you. Use the following road map to move on down the road in your career planning adventure.

Make two lists. On the first, list the things you like most about the career you are currently investigating. On the second, list the things that are most important to you in a future career. Look for similarities on both lists and focus on careers that emphasize these similar key points.

	Current Career		Future Career
☼	_____	☼	_____
☼	_____	☼	_____

What are some career ideas that are similar to the one you have in mind? Find out all you can about them. Go back through the exploration process explained on pages 161 to 170 and repeat some of the exercises that were most valuable.

☼ _____

☼ _____

☼ WRITE YOUR RESPONSES ON

☼ A SEPARATE PIECE OF PAPER

Visit your school counselor and ask him or her which career assessment tools are available through your school. Use these to find out more about your strengths and interests. List the date, time, and place for any assessment tests you plan to take.

WRITE YOUR RESPONSES ON A SEPARATE PIECE OF PAPER

What other adults do you know and respect to whom you can talk about your future? They may have ideas that you've never thought of.

WRITE YOUR RESPONSES ON A SEPARATE PIECE OF PAPER

What kinds of part-time jobs, volunteer work, or after-school experiences can you look into that will give you a chance to build your skills and test your abilities? Think about how you can tap into these opportunities.

WRITE YOUR RESPONSES ON A SEPARATE PIECE OF PAPER

GREEN LIGHT

Yahoo! You are totally turned on to this career idea and ready to do whatever it takes to make it your life's work. Go for it!

Find out what kinds of classes you need to take now to prepare for this career. List them here.

WRITE YOUR RESPONSES ON A SEPARATE PIECE OF PAPER

What are some on-the-job training possibilities for you to pursue? List the company name, a person to contact, and the phone number.

- ☼ _____
- ☼ _____
- ☼ _____
- ☼ _____

WRITE YOUR RESPONSES ON A SEPARATE PIECE OF PAPER

Find out if there are any internship or apprenticeship opportunities available in this career field. List contacts and phone numbers.

- ☼ _____
- ☼ _____
- ☼ _____
- ☼ _____

WRITE YOUR RESPONSES ON A SEPARATE PIECE OF PAPER

What kind of education will you need after you graduate from high school? Describe the options.

- ☼ _____
- ☼ _____
- ☼ _____
- ☼ _____

WRITE YOUR RESPONSES ON A SEPARATE PIECE OF PAPER

No matter what the educational requirements are, the better your grades are during junior and senior high school, the better your chances for the future.

Take a minute to think about some areas that need improvement in your schoolwork. Write your goals for giving it all you've got here.

- ☼ _____
- ☼ _____
- ☼ _____
- ☼ _____

WRITE YOUR RESPONSES ON A SEPARATE PIECE OF PAPER

Where can you get the training you'll need? Make a list of colleges, technical schools, or vocational programs. Include addresses so that you can write to request a catalog.

WRITE YOUR RESPONSES ON A SEPARATE PIECE OF PAPER

HOORAY! YOU DID IT!

This has been quite a trip. If someone tries to tell you that this process is easy, don't believe it. Figuring out what you want to do with the rest of your life is heavy stuff, and it should be. If you don't put some thought (and some sweat and hard work) into the process, you'll get stuck with whatever comes your way.

You may not have things planned to a T. Actually, it's probably better if you don't. You'll change some of your ideas as you grow and experience new things. And, you may find an interesting detour or two along the way. That's OK.

The most important thing about beginning this process now is that you've started to dream. You've discovered that you have some unique talents and abilities to share. You've become aware of some of the ways you can use them to make a living—and, perhaps, make a difference in the world.

Whatever you do, don't lose sight of the hopes and dreams you've discovered. You've got your entire future ahead of you. Use it wisely.

SOME FUTURE DESTINATIONS

Wow! You've really made tracks during this whole process. Now that you've gotten this far, you'll want to keep moving forward to a great future. This section will point you toward some useful resources to help you make a conscientious career choice (that's just the opposite of falling into any old job on a fluke).

IT'S NOT JUST FOR NERDS

The school counselor's office is not just a place where teachers send troublemakers. One of its main purposes is to help students like you make the most of your educational opportunities. Most schools will have a number of useful resources, including career assessment tools (ask about the Self-Directed Search Career Explorer or the COPS Interest Inventory—these are especially useful assessments for people your age). There may also be a stash of books, videos, and other helpful materials.

Make sure no one's looking and sneak into your school counseling office to get some expert advice!

AWESOME INTERNET CAREER RESOURCES

Your parents will be green with envy when they see all the career planning resources you have at your fingertips. Get ready to hear them whine, "But they didn't have all this stuff when I was a kid." Make the most of these cyberspace opportunities.

- ☿ Future Scan includes in-depth profiles on a wide variety of career choices and expert advice from their "Guidance Gurus." Check it out at http://www.futurescan.com.
- ☿ For up-to-the-minute news on what's happening in the world of work, visit Career Magazine's website at http://www.careermag.com.
- ☿ Monster.com, one of the web's largest job search resources, hosts a site called Monster Campus at http://campus.monster.com. There's all kinds of career information, college stuff, and links to jobs, jobs, jobs!
- ☿ Find links to all kinds of career information at http://careerplanning.about.com. You'll have to use your best detective skills to find what you want, but there is a lot of good information to be found on this site.

☼ Even Uncle Sam wants to help you find a great career. Check out the Department of Labor's Occupational Outlook Handbook for in-depth information on approximately 250 occupations at http://www.bls.gov/ocohome.htm.

☼ Another fun site for the inside scoop on a wide variety of career options is found at http://www.jobprofiles.com.

☼ Pick a favorite career and find out specific kinds of information such as wages and trends at http://www.acinet.org/acinet

IT'S NOT JUST FOR BOYS

Boys and girls alike are encouraged to contact their local version of the Boy Scouts Explorer program. It offers exciting on-the-job training experiences in a variety of professional fields. Look in the white pages of your community phone book for the local Boy Scouts of America program.

MORE BOOKS ABOUT MONEYMAKING CAREER IDEAS

If making money is your aim, the world of business is your game. For more ideas on finding a future that pays off, thumb through some of the following books.

Field, Shelley. *100 Best Careers for the 21st Century*. Indianapolis: IDG Books Worldwide, 1996.

Harbavy, Michael David. *101 Careers: A Guide to the Fastest-Growing Opportunities*. New York: John Wiley, 1998.

Krannich, Ronald L., and Caryl Rae Krannich. *The Best Jobs for the 21st Century*. Manassas, Va.: Impact Publications, 1998.

Wright, John. *The American Almanac of Jobs and Salaries*. New York: Avon Books, 2000.

Yates, Martin. *Career Smarts: Jobs with a Future*. New York: Ballantine, 1997.

HEAVY-DUTY RESOURCES

Career encyclopedias provide general information about a lot of professions and can be a great place to start a career search. Those listed here are easy to use and provide useful information about nearly a zillion different jobs. Look for them in the reference section of your local library.

Cosgove, Holli, ed. *Career Discovery Encyclopedia: 2000 Edition.* Chicago: J.G. Ferguson Publishing Company, 2000.

Hopke, William. *Encyclopedia of Careers and Vocational Guidance.* Chicago: J.G. Ferguson Publishing Company, 1999.

Maze, Marilyn, Donald Mayall, and J. Michael Farr. *The Enhanced Guide for Occupational Exploration: Descriptions for the 2,800 Most Important Jobs.* Indianapolis: JIST Works, 1995.

VGM's Career Encyclopedia. Lincolnwood, Ill.: VGM Career Books, 1997.

FINDING PLACES TO WORK

Use resources like these to find leads on local businesses, mentors, job shadowing opportunities, and internships. Later, use these same resources to find a great job!

Cubbage, Sue A. *National Job Hotline Directory.* River Forest, Ill.: Planning/Communications, 1998.

Graber, Steve. *Adams Jobs Almanac.* Holbrooke, Mass.: Adams Media, 1998.

———. *The Job Bank Guide to Computer and High Tech Companies.* Holbrooke, Mass.: Adams Media, 1997.

Levering, Robert. *100 Best Companies to Work for in America.* New York: Plume, 1994.

Peterson's Hidden Job Market. Princeton, N.J.: Peterson's Guides, 1998.

Peterson's Top 2500 Employers. Princeton, N.J.: Peterson's Guides, 1999.

Plunkett, Jack W. *The Almanac of American Employers.* Houston: Plunkett Research, 2000.

Potts, Kathleen E. Maki, ed. *Job Hunter's Sourcebook: Where to Find Employment Leads and Other Job Search Resources.* Detroit: Gale, 1999.

U.S. Department of Labor's Career Guide to America's Top Industries. Indianapolis: JIST Works, 1998.

Also consult the Job Bank series (Holbrook, Mass.: Adams Media Group). Adams publishes separate guides for Atlanta, Seattle, and many major points in between. Ask your local librarian if the library has a guide for the biggest city near you.

FINDING PLACES TO PRACTICE JOB SKILLS

An apprenticeship is an official opportunity to learn a specific profession by working side by side with a skilled professional. As a training method, it's as old as the hills, and it's making a comeback in a big way because people are realizing that doing a job is simply the best way to learn a job.

An internship is an official opportunity to gain work experience (paid or unpaid) in an industry of interest. Interns are more likely to be given entry-level tasks but often have the chance to rub elbows with people in key positions within a company. In comparison to an apprenticeship, which offers very detailed training for a specific job, an internship offers a broader look at a particular kind of work environment.

Both are great ways to learn the ropes and stay one step ahead of the competition. Consider it dress rehearsal for the real thing!

Anselm, John. *The Yale Daily News Guide to Internships*. New York: Kaplan, 1999.

Oakes, Elizabeth H. *Ferguson's Guide to Apprenticeship Programs*. Chicago: J.G. Ferguson Publishing Company, 1998.

Oldman, Mark. *America's Top Internships*. New York: Princeton Review, 1999.

Peterson's Internships 2000. Princeton, N.J.: Peterson's Guides, 1999.

NO-COLLEGE OCCUPATIONS

Some of you will be relieved to learn that a college degree is not the only route to a satisfying, well-paying career. Whew! If you'd rather skip some of the schooling and get down to work, here are some books you need to consult.

Abrams, Kathleen S. *Guide to Careers Without College*. Danbury, Conn.: Franklin Watts, 1995.

Corwen, Leonard. *College Not Required: 100 Great Careers That Don't Require a College Degree*. New York: Macmillan, 1995.

Farr, J. Michael. *America's Top Jobs for People Without College Degrees*. Indianapolis: JIST Works, 1998.

Unger, Harlow G. *But What If I Don't Want to Go to College?: A Guide to Successful Careers through Alternative Education*. New York: Facts On File, 1998.

INDEX

Page numbers in **boldface** indicate main articles. Page numbers in *italics* indicate photographs.